FROM MEDIEVAL MANUSCRIPT TO MODERN PRACTICE

The Wrestling Techniques of Fiore dei Liberi

GUY WINDSOR

From Medieval Manuscript to Modern Practice: The Wrestling Techniques of Fiore dei Liberi

Publisher: Spada Press, Helsinki, Finland
© Guy Windsor 2024
www.swordschool.com

ISBN 978-952-7157-34-3 From Medieval Manuscript to Modern Practice:
The Wrestling Techniques of Fiore dei Liberi (hardback)
ISBN 978-952-7157-35-0 From Medieval Manuscript to Modern Practice:
The Wrestling Techniques of Fiore dei Liberi (paperback)
ISBN 978-952-7157-36-7 From Medieval Manuscript to Modern Practice:
The Wrestling Techniques of Fiore dei Liberi (ebook)

Book and cover design by Zebedee Design

TABLE OF CONTENTS

INTRODUCTION

Sometime in the late 14th century, a master of knightly combat wrote a treatise that presents a complete vision of the art of arms as he saw it. His name was Fiore dei Liberi, and his treatise is called *Il Fior di Battaglia*, 'The Flower of Battle'. His work exists in four known manuscript versions, which cover the range of knightly weapons including sword, lance, pollax and dagger, on foot and on horseback, in armour and out of armour, as well as wrestling and other weapon combinations. In this book we will look at his introduction, and wrestling material out of armour and on foot. Before we dive in I should answer a few questions that may have occurred to you:

- What can I expect from this book?
- Who was Fiore and why should we take him seriously?
- What are these four manuscripts, and how should we approach them?
- Who is this Guy Windsor fellow and why should I trust his interpretation?

Ready? Let's go.

About this book

In many respects this book is a new kind of academic work, in which I present my transcription and translation of the source material, comment on it, and present video examples of how I enact the content. It began as The Fiore Translation Project, a series of blog posts in which I translate and comment on *Il Fior di Battaglia*, the treatise written by Fiore dei Liberi, arguably the greatest master of knightly combat instruction of the fourteenth century. I began with the Longsword plays, which were published as *From Medieval Manuscript to Modern Practice: The Longsword Techniques of Fiore dei Liberi*, in 2020. I hope to produce equivalent books for the entire treatise, adding volumes on the dagger, the armoured plays on foot, and the mounted plays, in due course. Time will tell whether I get around to it – but if you write and let me know you really want me to, that will make it more likely.

I have chosen to release the transcription and translation under a Creative Commons Attribution licence. You may do anything you like with that material, so long as you acknowledge where it came from. The commentary and video footage remain under my copyright.

Video links are included so that you can see how I do the actions Fiore described. These links are embedded in electronic versions of this book, and expanded so you can type them into a browser if you are using the print version. You can also find all the videos collected in one place for your convenience at this page on my website:

https://guywindsor.net/fiorewrestlingvideos

These are not instructional videos, and if you choose to try things out it's entirely at your own risk. I take no responsibility for you unless you are under my direct supervision. This book will lay out for you how I think Fiore's wrestling plays work, and why I think they are like that. It's academic, and intended to present my interpretation in the most robust way. You will see what I think Fiore wrote (the transcription), what I think his Italian means in English (the translation), and how I enact those words in practice (the commentary and video clips). But this is not a training manual—I'm not trying to teach you how to do these plays, nor to develop your wrestling skills. For that, I have an online course (co-hosted by Jessica Finley) that you can find at guywindsor.net/abrazarecourse. All of the video clips in this book are extracted from that course. It is simply much more effective to teach skills through video than through text.

The genesis of this book (and its predecessor) was in Seattle, where I had a conversation with the excellent Michael Chidester, known for his work on the wonderful web archive of fencing treatises Wiktenauer. com, and we agreed that the world needs a new, free translation of Fiore's Getty MS. There is nothing wrong with the current published translation by Tom Leoni, but a) it isn't free and b) in the interests of making the translation very clear, Tom tends towards oversimplifying the text.

This is a huge project. I knew when I began it that if I started at the beginning (the introduction), and worked my way steadily through the whole book, I'd get stuck, lose interest, and the project would fail. It's too big. So I decided to go through the bits I was most interested in first, and transcribe, translate, and comment on them as I went. My aim was to transcribe and translate the related sections of the other Fiorean manuscripts at the same time, as the whimsy took me. This has hopefully generated a lot of useful material for scholars of the art.

My process has been simple: I transcribe one paragraph of Fiore's text, straight from the manuscript, and translate it, make whatever comments seem interesting and relevant to me, such as cross-references with other parts of the book, notes from my own experience and so on, then move on to the next paragraph. At the end of each section I comment on the section as a whole, and say how I think it fits into the rest of the book, the other manuscripts, and any related texts and systems.

The transcription is not supposed to be flawless, just clear enough so that where the text could be transcribed in more than one way, you can see which I've chosen. I have not modernised the text in terms of spelling or accents, but I have distinguished between *che* (that) and *ch'e* (that is) in the transcription. I have expanded all contractions and abbreviations as well, but not worried too much about the punctuation.

Fiore uses it quite inconsistently anyway, so I have added commas and full stops where I think they belong. I have also included accidental repeats of words, crossed-out words, and other errors, because they're interesting. It's not my job to correct the master. The purpose of including the transcription is to make it clear how I'm reading the book, which informs how I have translated it.

It would be both academically unsound and foolish not to make use of the existing translations and transcriptions, so when called for I have checked the Wiktenauer transcriptions and translation (by Colin Hatcher and Michael Chidester), and Tom Leoni's, to see how they have solved the problem. I don't always agree, of course, but you should be aware that this project owes a debt to their work.

Readers of *The Theory and Practice of Historical Martial Arts* may recall that I have a particular way of approaching fencing sources, which includes establishing three contexts that the source exists in: the historical context, the fencing context, and the martial context. I also like to create an annotated table of contents of the entire source, as a way of getting to grips with the overall context that the source creates for any given action described within it. Let's take a look at those contexts (this is borrowed with minor adjustments from *From Medieval Manuscript to Modern Practice: The Longsword Techniques of Fiore dei Liberi*).

Historical Context: The who? where? and when? of Fiore dei Liberi

Fiore dei Liberi was a master of the art of arms (which he called *armizare*). He was born some time around 1350, and died some time after 1410. Most of what we know about his life comes from the introduction to his manuscripts, and from research done by Francesco Novati (who published the Pisani-Dossi manuscript in facsimile in 1902) and Luigi Zanutto (who published *Fiore dei Liberi da Premariacco e i ludi e le festi marziali in Friuli nel Medio-evo* in 1907). Dr Ken Mondschein has published an excellent summary of Fiore's life based on the manuscripts and these two early 20th century sources in his book *The Knightly Art of Battle* and his open source (i.e. free!) article 'On the Art of Fighting: A Humanist Translation of Fiore dei Liberi's Flower of Battle Owned by Leonello D'Este'. I highly recommend both, and am drawing on them for this summary of what we know.

The first lines of the Getty manuscript are:

*Fior Furlan de Civida d'ostria che fo di misser Benedetto de la
nobel casada deli liberi da Premeryas d'la dyocesi dello
Patriarchado de Aquilegia in sua coventu volse inprender ad
armizare e arte de combatter in sbarra...*

Fior the Friulian from Cividale in Austria, son of the late Ser
Benedetto of the noble house of Liberi of Premariacco in the
diocese of the Patriarch of Aquileia from his youth wanted to learn
the art of arms and the art of combat in the lists...

Let's unpack that name, shall we? We know the author as Fiore dei
Liberi, but that's not exactly how he introduces himself. Firstly, it was
normal for non-noble families to be named after the place in which
they were born. The most famous example is perhaps Leonardo da
Vinci: Vinci is just a town not far from Florence.

Friuli is an area in north-east Italy, bordering on Austria to the
North, Slovenia to the East, and the Veneto to the West and South. It
was initially created as a Lombard Duchy, and it has always had a
very clear cultural identity, so no wonder Fiore identifies himself as
Friulian. Cividale is a town close to the Slovenian border, and
Premariacco is a village just outside Cividale. So it would seem that
his family was from Premariacco, but his home town was Cividale.
Fiore was famous enough in his time that there are streets named after
him in Cividale, Premariacco, and even Udine (the major city to the
west of Cividale where Fiore lived and worked later in life).

The Patriarchate of Aquileia is the Church see (an area overseen by
a bishop), with its episcopal headquarters in Aquileia, a town on the
Adriatic coast about 40 km to the South of Cividale. So Fiore is being
careful to locate himself firmly in terms of political region (Friuli),
episcopal region (Aquileia), home town (Cividale), and social rank (son
of a knight, from a specific town, Premariacco), with a particular
surname (Liberi).

In the Pisani-Dossi manuscript he states that he is writing on 10

February 1409, which would be 1410 by the modern calendar,[1] and that he had been training for 50 years. This means he would have begun training in about 1360, and the usual age for boys of the knightly classes to begin training was about ten, putting his date of birth some time around 1350. Incidentally, in the Getty manuscript he claims 40 years of experience, suggesting that it was written in about 1400. This matches his reference to Galeazzo da Mantoa as a student: Galeazzo was a very famous *condottiere* (mercenary captain), who died at the siege of Medolago in 1406 – if he was known to be dead at the time of writing, it would probably be mentioned in the text.

This fits with what we know of Fiore's career: he was granted residency in the city of Udine on 3 August 1383, and in September that year he was commissioned to inspect and repair the crossbows and siege engines of the Udine arsenal. In May 1384 he appears in the Udine records as "Fiore the fencing master", and was in effect a magistrate, being assigned to Gemona, about 25 km to the North of Udine.

He names many of his students in the manuscripts, which I think we can take at face value, because these men would have been known to the likely readership, and so false claims would have been easily spotted. I recommend Mondschein's article as the place to go for a thorough description of those students.

The Getty and Pisani-Dossi manuscripts are both dedicated to Niccolò III d'Este, Marquis of Ferrara. Niccolò was born in 1383 and died in 1441, at the age of 10 becoming the Marquis on the death of his father Alberto in 1393. Born illegitimate, he was something of a player and a hypocrite – he had his wife and his illegitimate son Ugo executed for adultery, while nonetheless fathering at least 11 illegitimate children. He was married three times, and had five legitimate children too. Dedicating his work to the Marquis was no doubt a smart move on Fiore's part, as, especially towards the end of his life, he would have been in need of patronage. Whether he was successful or not we

---

1   Beginning in 1582, most European countries shifted from the Julian Calendar to the Gregorian. This process was haphazard: Britain changed over in 1752, Russia in 1918, and also entailed a correction. In Britain this was of eleven days: Wednesday 2 September 1752 was followed by Thursday 14 September! For our purposes, it's clear enough that Fiore was writing in February 1410 by our reckoning.

don't know, but it's interesting that the last words in the Getty manuscript are:

> *Qui finisse lo libro che a fatto lo scolaro Fiore che zo ch'ello sa in quest'arte qui l'a posto, zoe in tutto la armizare in questo libro e lo fiore Fiore di Bataglia per nome ello e chiamato. Quello per chi ello e fatto sempre sia apresiato che di nobilita e virtu se trova lo parechio. Fior furlan a voy si recomanda povero vechio.*

> Here ends the book that was made by the scholar Fiore, in which is that which he knows of this art, thus the flower of the entire art of arms is in this book, called by name the Flower of Battle. The one for whom it is made should always be praised, who is the example of nobility and virtue. Fior the Friulian to you recommends himself, a poor old man.

So he ends with some fluffy praise, both for his book and his quondam patron. Perhaps my favourite place where Fiore addresses Niccolò directly is on folio 37v of the Getty manuscript (more about that later), where he describes a pollax that has poison dust in the head.

Questa mia Azza era prena de poluere, e se
la dicta Azza bufada in tono i torno. e questa poluere
si fose cörosiua che subito come ella tocha lochio, l'omo p
nullun modo nol po auere, e fuorsi mai no uedera piu.
Azza son ponderosa crudele e mortale. mazori colpi
fazo che altra arma manuale. E se io falisso lo pmo colpo
che uegno afare, la Azza me dä danno e niente piu non
uale. E se io fiero lo pmo colpo ch'io fazzo, tutte le altre
arme manuale io cauo d'inpazo. E se son cü bone arme
ben acompagnada, p mia dofesa piglio le guarde,
pulsatiue de spada. Signore nobilissimo Signor
mio marchese, assay chose sono in questo libro che uoi
tale malicie no le fareste. ma p piu sauere, piaza
ui di uederle.

Questa e la poluere che uai i la Azza penta q sop.
Pigla la latte delo titimallo, e seccalo al sole ouero
in forno caldo e fane poluere, e piglia di questa
poluere unc. ij. e una onza de poluere d'fior de
preda, e mestola i sembre, e questa poluere si de
metter in la azza qui de sopra, beñ che se po fare
cü ogni ritorio che sia fino, che ben ne trouereti
di fini in questo libro.

This sort of dirty trick is not standard knightly behaviour, so Fiore writes:

> *Signore, nobilissimo signor, mio Marchese, assay chose sono in questo libro che voy tale malicie non le fareste. Ma per piu savere piazavi di vederle.*
>
> Sir, most noble sir, my Marquis, there are things in this book of such malice that you would not do them. But for the sake of knowledge it may please you to see them.

He then goes on to give us the recipe![2]

Niccolò was appointed *Gonfaloniere della Chiesa* by Pope Boniface IX in 1403. Literally 'Bannerman of the Church', this was effectively commander of the Papal armies, and the highest military honour available in the Papal States. If you imagine Italy as a thigh-high boot kicking the football that is Sicily, from the toe to just below the knee was the Kingdom of Naples. The Papal States ran from the knee to mid-thigh, and up the back of the leg as far north as Ferrara. It was a significant chunk of the Italian peninsular, and the largest single dominion after Naples. As for the rest of the peninsular, it was primarily divided into the Duchy of Milan, which controlled much of the north, and the Maritime States around the edges, chiefly Genoa and Pisa in the west, and Venice to the east, with Florence, Siena, Verona, and Lucca all powerful and important independent city states further inland. It's worth remembering that Italy did not become one nation until the Risorgimento, officially dated to 1861, but the last gasp of the civil wars that lead to final unification was (probably) the capture of Rome in 1870.

To compound the problem of these various city states, Papal states, and independent kingdoms all trying to expand their borders, within every state there was usually a division between Guelphs and Ghibellines: Guelphs supporting the Pope, and Ghibellines the Holy Roman Emperor.

Confused? You're not alone. I started writing this brief historical

---

2   See https://guywindsor.net/2014/05/blinded-by-botany-medieval-malice/ for details.

overview by compiling a map of the independent states in Italy in 1400, and gave it up after many hours because it would be accurate for one specific day in one specific year only. And probably not particularly accurate at that. The borders were constantly changing, and so were the alliances, and influences from abroad. Let's have a brief look at some of those external influences at work during Fiore's time.

The Holy Roman Empire was neither Holy, Roman, nor really an empire, but a loose confederation of mostly Germanic states. The terms Guelph and Ghibelline are italicised versions of German names. The Empire began with Charlemagne being crowned by Pope Leo III in 800ACE. Fiore was born during the reign of Emperor Charles IV, who died in 1378 and was succeeded by his son Sigismund. Fiore's birthplace is very close to the borders of the Empire, and it's telling that Fiore notes in his introduction that he studied under both German and Italian masters.

The French were also involved in Italian affairs. Aragon was especially important because from 1309 to 1377 there was a second Pope, known as the "antipope", further dividing loyalties. Leaving religion aside for a moment, Sicily was under the Aragonese crown from the mid-13th century until 1409.

And we mustn't forget the English. In 1345 Edward III defaulted on his Crown debts to the Florentine banks of Bardi and Peruzzi, which both collapsed. This caused a kind of recession, not helped by the Plague which ravaged Florence and much of the rest of Tuscany from 1345-1351. Sir John Hawkwood (ca 1323-1394), one of the best-known *condottiere* of the 14th century, made a fortune working as a mercenary. He began his military life probably as a bowman, before joining the White Company (a mercenary troop), swiftly rising to command it. Fiore would have certainly known of him, though there's no evidence I'm aware of that they ever met.

It would take many volumes of dense research to draw a complete picture of what was going on politically and militarily in Fiore's lifetime. The various states within Italy were continually renegotiating their borders with each other, creating and breaking alliances, and being affected by foreign influences. To find out more about any of these topics, I suggest searching Wikipedia for the keyword that strikes your curiosity (such as "Ghibelline"), reading the articles that pop up, and trawling through the references at the bottom of each entry for book and article recommendations if you want to go deeper. If you prefer fiction, the series of historical novels by Christian Cameron beginning with *The Ill-Made Knight* are impeccably researched, and will give you a broader picture of what was going on militarily during Fiore's lifetime: the master himself even appears as a character!

For our purposes, it's enough to know that there was always a military action going on somewhere in the Italian peninsular, and the skills Fiore taught were in high demand because a great deal of the action was fought with the classic weapons of knightly combat – sword, dagger, lance and axe, on foot and mounted, in armour and without.

In summary then, we can take his book seriously as a martial arts resource because the man who wrote it was a skilled and respected military person, who could claim some of the greatest warriors of the age as his students in the art of arms, and who was sufficiently widely respected that he could reasonably expect the Marquis of Ferrara to actually read his book.

THE FENCING CONTEXT

I visualise fencing context as a cross, with our target source in the middle, prior sources (if relevant) below, contemporary sources to either side, and later sources above.

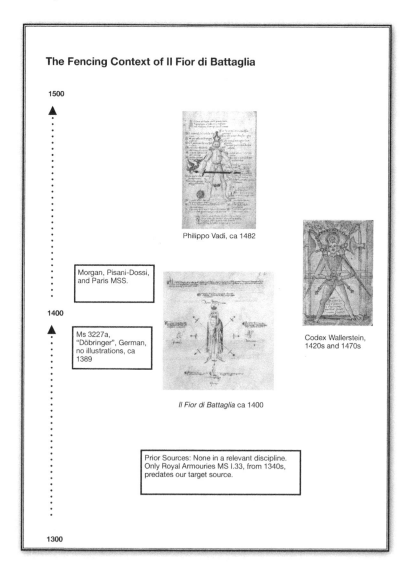

The Fencing Context of Il Fior di Battaglia

1500

Philippo Vadi, ca 1482

Morgan, Pisani-Dossi, and Paris MSS.

1400

Ms 3227a, "Döbringer", German, no illustrations, ca 1389

Codex Wallerstein, 1420s and 1470s

Il Fior di Battaglia ca 1400

Prior Sources: None in a relevant discipline. Only Royal Armouries MS I.33, from 1340s, predates our target source.

1300

Prior sources

As you can see, there are no prior sources for *Il Fior di Battaglia*; the only fencing source that is reliably dated to before ours is a German sword and buckler manual, Royal Armouries MS I.33. There doesn't seem to be any relevant connection between them in terms of fencing style or martial context. Ideally we would have at least a few prior sources to draw on, as it can be very helpful in the interpretation process to see what came before: what has been kept, what has been changed, and what has been rejected. Some sources are in explicit disagreement with their predecessors.

Contemporary Sources

We do at least have some contemporary sources. There are at least a few German manuscripts from the late 1300s or early 1400s, which may show us how other people (perhaps even Fiore's "German masters") were wrestling at about the same time. You should at least be aware of these sources, and in an ideal world would read them, discuss their contents with scholars studying them, and if you are actively recreating Fiore's style, then you should also cross-train in the early German styles. You don't need to be expert in them, but you should be aware of what else was going on in the fencing world at that time. Assuming you don't read German, I suggest beginning with Jessica Finley's *Medieval Wrestling: modern practice of a fifteenth century art,* published in 2014. From there, you can go deep into the German sources with any of Christian Tobler's works, as well those of Dierk Hagedorn (such as *Jude Lew*) and Hagedorn with Bartolomiej Walczak (such as *Gladiatoria*), or Walczak with Grzegorz Zabinski (*Codex Wallerstein*).

   In Fiore's case, there are four versions of his manuscript that we know of, all of which were written within a fairly short space of time (perhaps 30 years). These are obviously the most important contemporary sources, and I will go into them in some detail below.

Later sources

There are many, many, sources that came after Fiore. In this context cross I've chosen just one, Philippo Vadi's *De Arte Gladiatoria Dimicandi,* which has clear links to Fiore (which I discuss in detail in

The Art of Sword Fighting in Earnest). While Vadi doesn't address wrestling, he does include a lot of dagger plays. If we didn't have Vadi's MS, we would probably fill out that top section with Bolognese sources such as Manciolino's *Opera Nova* from 1531. It is useful but not strictly necessary to train in the later styles. "Not necessary" because they can't have influenced Fiore. Academically, it's essential that you become familiar with the later sources because they often shed useful light on the prior ones. For instance, terminology that is undefined in one source may be defined elsewhere (and its meaning may not have changed in the time elapsed).

If at this point you are reeling in shock at the combined cost of your new reading list, let me remind you that practically all of these books can be ordered from your local library, at no cost at all.

THE FOUR VERSIONS OF THE TREATISE

In the case of Fiore's treatise we are truly spoiled in that we have four surviving manuscript copies that have surfaced so far. There may even be more! In cases like this we need to know everything we can find out about each copy, then choose one to focus on. The four copies of Fiore's manuscripts are:

Il Fior di Battaglia (MS Ludwig XV13), held in the J.P. Getty museum in Los Angeles. The 'Getty', as it is generally known, covers wrestling, dagger, dagger against sword, longsword, sword in armour, pollax, spear, lance on horseback, sword on horseback and wrestling on horseback. The text includes detailed instructions for the plays. Regarding dating, in this manuscript Fiore mentions a duel between Galeazzo da Mantoa and Jean le Maingre (Boucicault), which we know took place in 1395. He does not mention Galeazzo's death, which occurred in 1406 (a crossbow bolt in the eye at Medolago). So it seems likely that the manuscript was written between 1395 and 1406. The treatise was published in facsimile by Massimo Malipiero in 2006, and a full translation into English was published by Tom Leoni in 2009. It has recently been re-translated, with an extensive introduction, as *Flowers of Battle Volume 1*, by Tom Leoni and Gregory Mele, which is a must-have book for all Fiore scholars.

Flos Duellatorum, is in private hands in Italy, and was published in facsimile in 1902 by Francesco Novati. The 'Novati' or the 'Pisani-Dossi' follows more or less the same order and has more or less the same content as the Getty. The main differences are that the spear section comes between the dagger and the sword, and the dagger against sword material is at the end. The text is generally far less specific than in the Getty, but it is the only version that is dated by the author, who states that he is writing on 10 February 1409 (1410 by modern reckoning).

Il Fior di Battaglia (Morgan MS M 383), the 'Morgan', held in the Pierpont Morgan museum in New York, proceeds more like a passage of arms: first comes mounted combat with lance, with sword, and unarmed; then on foot with spear, sword in armour, sword out of armour, and sword against dagger. There is no wrestling or dagger combat shown except against a sword, though they are mentioned in the introduction. I conclude that the manuscript is incomplete. Most of the specific plays shown here are also in the Getty, and these have almost identical texts.

Florius de Arte Luctandi (MSS LATIN 11269), recently discovered in the Bibliothèque Nationale de France in Paris, is probably a later copy. 'Florius' has Latin text and is beautifully coloured. It follows the approximate order of the Morgan, though is more complete, containing all the sections seen in the Getty and the Novati.

You can find scans of all of these manuscripts at the amazing Wiktenauer.com.

There is a cadre of Fiore scholars who remember the bad old days when a very poor photocopy of the Pisani-Dossi MS , with extremely bad English translations pasted over the original text, was the ONLY version of *Il Fior di Battaglia* that we had.

Seriously. That was it.

No wonder we struggled. I first saw this in 1994, and felt totally justified in keeping smallsword as my main focus. By the early 2000s, we had heard of the Getty, but it was almost impossible to see a copy. I blagged some not-very-clear scans in 2003, and better ones in 2005. In 2006 we saw full-res scans for the first time, when Brian Stokes gave a lecture on them at the WMAW event in Dallas. Oh my, did we get excited. We saw the first microfilmed scans of the Morgan in about 2002, and better images became available by about 2010. As for the Pisani-Dossi, a decent quality un-messed-about-with PDF became available in about 2002. Florius was discovered in 2008 independently by Ken Mondschein and Fabrice Cognot.

So which manuscript should we focus on? Most scholars working on Fiore agree that the Getty is the most useful source, since it is as complete as any other, and has the fuller, more explanatory text. My goal in studying Fiore is primarily to understand how sword fights work. I am a martial artist first, historian second. From that perspective, it makes sense to focus on the most complete version of the book (which would rule out the Morgan), with the best illustrations and the most complete, explanatory text. The Getty is the only sensible choice.

But, and this is a very large but, it would be very foolish not to take advantage of the other sources. Here's how I see them:

The Morgan

The first thing to note is that the Morgan starts with the lance on horseback, and proceeds in reverse order to the Getty. This means the book is following the order of a passage of arms, rather than the (probably) best pedagogical order.

It is also sadly incomplete. Though the introduction mentions dagger, for example, the book ends at the play of the sword in one hand.

The MS has been rebound out of order. I would order it like so: Folia 1–14 are correct. There's a page missing after 14, then the order should go: 16, 15, 18, 17, page missing, 19, rest of MS missing if it ever existed.

Where we have the same plays and actions, the text for the Morgan is remarkably similar to the Getty. To my mind the Morgan is principally useful for the one key theoretical insight it offers: the play of the sword on horseback showing the crossing of the swords, and this text:

Quisti doi magistri sono aqui incrosadi a tuta spada. E zoche po far uno por far l'altro, zoe che po fare tuti zoghi de spada cum lo incrosar. Ma lo incrosar sie de tre rafone, zoe a tuta spada e punta de spada. E chi e incrosado a tuta spada pocho gle po stare. E chi'e incrosado a meza spada meno gle po stare. E chi a punta de spada niente gle po stare. Si che la spada si ha in si tre cose, zoe, pocho, meno, e niente.

These two masters are here crossed *a tuta spada* ("at the whole sword"). And what one can do the other can do, thus [they] can do all the plays of the sword with the crossing. But the crossing is of three kinds, thus *a tuta spada* ("at the whole sword") and *a punta de spada* ("at the point of the sword"). [Note the inconsistency here: he says 'of three kinds', but mentions only two at this point.] And he who is crossed *a tuta spada*, little can he stand. And he who is crossed *a meza spada* (at the middle of the sword), less can he stand. And he who is crossed *a punta de spada*, nothing can he stand. So the sword has three things in it, thus: little, less, and nothing.

This is of course a matter of leverage: when the crossing is near the hilt (*a tutta spada*), you have some strength, you can stand, withstand, support, or hold, a little. At the middle, less, and at the point, nothing. Please note, fencers with a more modern background (shall we say from 1550 onwards) will be leaping up and down in excitement because in more modern systems, generally featuring swords with more complex, hand-protecting hilts, parries are done with what Fiore would call the *tuta spada* against the *punta di spada*. Or what rapierists would call the *forte* against the *debole*, and smallswordists the *fort* against the *feeble* (or *foible*). But, please note, *in every single case where Fiore describes the blade relationship at the parry, he specifies middle to middle*. This is, I think, for two reasons. Firstly, with an open-hilted sword, you cannot afford to put your hand so close to the enemy blade – you must parry further down the sword. Secondly, parries are not done as gentle but firm closings of the line; they are *rebattimenti*, beating actions. The *tuta spada* is not moving fast enough to hit with enough force to beat the opponent's weapon aside.

The Florius

Ken Mondschein has published a paper on this manuscript, called On the Art of Fighting: A Humanist Translation of Fiore dei Liberi's Flower of Battle Owned by Leonello D'Este, here: https://bop.unibe.ch/apd/article/view/6867. This is one of those 'Fiore scholars, you have no choice, you have to read this' moments. It's basically everything we know about Fiore, his life, and a lot of fascinating insights into his patrons and milieu. Plus, it's even free. Go read it.

As I see it, the Florius is a very pretty, but not very useful, version of the book. I paid the Bibliothèque Nationale de France about a thousand euros for the scans (which I'm not allowed to share, because that institution has a draconian view of copyright, but they've now put them online – see above), and while I don't regret that, it didn't actually change a single thing I was doing in class. No new techniques or concepts. The artwork is stylised to the point where it's not a usable reference source, and the text is as short as and even less helpful than the Pisani-Dossi. As Ken wrote, "the Paris manuscript changes the source material so considerably, and in a manner so consistent with it originating in the court of Leonello d'Este, Marquis of Ferrara, that we must consider it almost a separate work." Scholars need to know about it, and study it to some degree, but martial artists can move swiftly on. Again, if I've missed something, let me know!

The Pisani-Dossi

You can download a high-quality scan of the 1902 edition of this manuscript from here: https://guywindsor.net/pisanidossi

To be clear, the version we are all working from is the facsimile made by Francesco Novati and published in 1902. The original is in the Pisani-Dossi family vault, and to date has been seen only by Brian Stokes, because it is basically impossible to arrange a viewing: it requires all the heirs of the family (who apparently do not get on) to be present for the vault to be opened. However, as far as we know, the facsimile is accurate (according to Brian).

This MS is as complete as the Getty, but as we will see in the discussion of the sword in one hand master, the text is much less useful generally. However, as we will also see there, it does include some illustrations and plays that add significant depth to our understanding. Especially noteworthy is the crossing of the sword in *zogho stretto* from the *roverso* side, shown here:

Questa e coverta de la riverssa mano
Per far zoghi de fortissimo ingano
This is a cover from the backhand side,
To make plays of the greatest trickery.

Per la coverta de la riverssa mano acqui to afato
De zogho streto e de ferire non fera guardito
By the cover of the backhand side I have got you here
You can't defend yourself against the close plays or the strikes.

I am also jolly fond of the third master of the dagger from this MS;
it has a gloriously fun disarm:

Qui comenca zoghi de mi riverssa zoghi forti
Per tali zoghi non savez asay ne sono morti
E li zoghi li mie scholari seguizano
E pur de parte riverssa comenzazano.

Here begin the plays of my strong backhand plays
By these plays you don't know how many have died,
And the plays of my scholars that follow
And only of the backhand side, they begin.

Per lo zogho del magistro la daga o guadagnada
E de ferirte te fazo grande derada.

By the play of the master I have gained the dagger
And by striking you I'll cause you great discombobulation.

Sorry, I couldn't resist. The non-technical smack-talk cries out for non-technical language play. *Derada* is not exactly discombobulation, but the sense is the same.

One of the principal reasons I include this play in my Dagger Disarm Flowdrill (https://guywindsor.net/disarmflowdrill) part of my basic syllabus for *armizare*, is to specifically refer to the Pisani-Dossi, to make sure all of my students are aware that there is more than one copy of the source.

Let me just make the point about the text very clear. Here is the Pisani-Dossi version of the exchange of the thrust:

> *Aquesto e de punta un crudelle schanbiar*
> *In l'arte piu falsa punta de questa non se po far.*
> *Tu me trasisti de punta e questa io to dada*
> *E piu seguro se po far schivando la strada.*

> Here is a cruel exchange of the thrust,
> In the art you cannot do a more false [deceptive] thrust than this,
> You came to strike me with a thrust and I did this to you,
> And [to be] more secure you can go avoiding [out of] the way.

And now the same play from the Getty MS.:

> *Questo zogho si chiama scambiar de punta e se fa per tal modo*
> *zoe. Quando uno te tra una punta subito acresse lo tuo pe ch'e*
> *denanci fora de strada e cum l'altro pe passa ala traversa anchora*
> *fora di strada traversando la sua spada cum cum gli toi brazzi bassi*
> *e cum la punta de la tua spada erta in lo volto o in lo petto com'e*
> *depento.*

> This play is called the exchange of thrust, and it is done like this, thus. When one strikes a thrust at you immediately advance your foot that is in front out of the way and with the other foot pass also out of the way, crossing his sword with your arms low and with the point of your sword up in the face or in the chest as is pictured.

You can see then that one is general, and the other very specific. If you want to know which foot to move where, there's only one MS that will tell you, and it is also complete.

So, for anyone wanting to recreate Fiore's art, there is only one sensible choice of source to focus on. But, and it's a big but, you should also be intimately familiar with the Pisani-Dossi and the Morgan, and at least aware of the existence of the Florius.

THE "TABLE OF CONTENTS": THE STRUCTURE OF IL FIOR DI BATTAGLIA

Il Fior di Battaglia is a vast and complex treatise, covering an enormous range of weapon combinations, techniques, counters, and fundamental concepts. As it was written around 1400, it comes from a different cultural and educational background from ours, one in which memory training was fundamental. As a result, the lack of theoretical discussion in the work, and the way the information is presented, can present stumbling blocks to the modern reader. The sheer amount of information is daunting, and as it is spread over some 90-odd sides of vellum (conventionally numbered 1 to 47 recto and verso), keeping the structure clear in your head as you read can be difficult, so I'll lay it out for you. The first three written sides (p. 3 recto and verso, p. 4 recto) are taken up with a text-only introduction. This covers the following points:

- A brief autobiography of Fiore himself
- A list of his more famous students and some of their feats of arms
- A brief discussion of the secret nature of the art, and Fiore's opinions about different modes of combat (fighting armoured in the lists versus fighting in arming doublets with sharp swords)
- A further description of Fiore's training, and his opinions regarding the necessity of books in general for mastering the art
- A connection of Fiore himself and the book with a higher authority (Niccolò, Marquis of Este), who commissioned the work
- An overview of the book and its didactic conventions, beginning with some background information on wrestling, and advice to the student on what is required
- Discussion of *poste* (the guard positions used in this art)
- A description of a crown and garter convention by which one can tell at a glance who is winning the fight in any given image.

This last is critically important to following what is going on in the treatise, so I'll expand on it here. The figures that begin each section are shown standing in guard, and wear a crown to indicate their masterly status. They are the "first masters". Following them are one or more "remedy masters" (also called the "second masters"), who illustrate a defence against an attack. Following each of them in turn are their scholars, identified by a garter, who execute the techniques that follow the previous master's remedy. After a scholar or master may come a "counter-remedy master" (the "third master"), wearing a crown and a garter, who illustrates the counter to the remedy master, or to one of the remedy master's scholars. Occasionally, there is a fourth master, who may be called the "counter-counter-remedy master", who wears the crown and garter too. Fiore specifies that most sequences don't get beyond the third master (i.e. the attack is met by the remedy, which the attacker counters), and it is perilous (perhaps because it is insecure) to go beyond three or four. This visual convention is unique to Fiore as far as we know, and makes it easy to be sure who is supposed to win from any illustrated position, and what stage of the fight (principle or guard; defence; counter to the defence; counter to the counter) is being shown. When reading the treatise, you can immediately identify who is winning in a given picture by his bling – the most bling wins!

The finish to the introduction is particularly interesting: "The coloured letters, the illustrations and the plays will show you all the art clearly enough for you to understand it." In other words, this book should be enough to transmit the art completely. A bold claim, and one that is borne out, I think, once the conventions are understood.

Weapon by weapon: the sections of the manuscript
The manuscript is divided into sections, which are linked together. The primary divisions (mentioned in the title of the Pisani-Dossi) are on foot, on horseback, in armour and out of armour. The secondary divisions are by weapon. We begin on foot, out of armour:

- *Abrazare*: wrestling. This has one remedy master, and a total of 20 plays. The first 16 are unarmed, then come two with a short stick (*bastoncello*), and two with the stick against the dagger, connecting us to

- Dagger: this is a huge section, with 76 plays, divided up amongst nine remedy masters. This is followed by defence of the dagger against the sword, and hence
- Sword in one hand: this contains one remedy master followed by 11 plays, which will be detailed later in this book. They lead us to
- The sword in two hands: this starts with a description of footwork, then six different ways to hold and use the sword, then 12 guards. The plays are divided into
  - *Zogho largo*, wide play: 20 plays, including two remedy masters
  - *Zogho stretto*, close play: 23 plays deriving from a single remedy master, which is followed by
  - Defence from sword guards on the left side – a single remedy master, with no scholars, who is followed by
  - Staff and dagger against spear, and two clubs and a dagger against spear. This seems to finish the unarmoured material (though some of the dagger plays require armour).

There follows:

- The segno page, or "seven swords"; a memory map for the system as a whole, and illustrating the four virtues required for success in the art.

From here on, we are mostly in armour:

- Sword in armour – six guard positions, one remedy master, one counter-remedy master, and a total of 16 plays
- Pollax – again six guard positions, eight plays with no specific remedy master, and two more showing variations on the axe: one with a weight on a rope, the other with a box of poison dust on the end. This is followed by the:
- Spear – first we see three guards on the right, one play and one counter-remedy, then three guards on the left, and one play.

And finally, mounted combat:

- Lance – five plays, each with their own master, including one counter-remedy
- Lance against sword – five plays, including three counter-remedies
- Sword – one guard position, shown against two attacks, with nine plays
- *Abrazare* – seven plays including three counter-remedies
- On foot with *ghiaverina*, a type of spear, against mounted opponents, one master followed by two plays
- Lance and rope – a last play of lance against lance, showing a specific trick for dismounting an opponent
- Sword against sword – a last, probably allegorical, play, in which you chase your opponent back to his castle, in which his villainous friends are waiting.

In this book we shall confine ourselves mostly to the *abrazare* section. This does not suggest that these sections are somehow a standalone treatise; on the contrary, understanding them has required many readings of the entire manuscript, and exhaustive recreation of the entire system on foot. The sections complement and reinforce each other: when a longsword pommel strike comes in, treat it like a dagger attack: when you end up too close to use your pollax, use the wrestling plays. There is much to learn about the spear from the plays of the sword, and so on.

In any given section there will usually be one or more "remedy masters" wearing a crown, illustrating the defence against a particular attack. These are followed by scholars, wearing a garter, who complete the play of the previous master. There are often also counter-remedy masters, wearing a crown and a garter, which counter either the scholar that comes before them, or the master himself. In other words their action may be specific to one scholar, or more generally applicable to the remedy itself.

The plays are the illustrations of the techniques, so we see a picture of a player (wearing no crown or garter) getting beaten by a master, scholar, or counter-remedy master. One technical sequence, such as a parry and strike, might take up one, two or three such illustrations, each of which is a play. As the term implies, there is often a lot of 'play' in the execution of these techniques, and several different ways to enter into a given play. Fiore scholars tend to keep the key plays in memory, in the order that they appear in the Getty MS It has become the norm to refer to the plays by their number – such as 'the third play of the second master of *zogho largo*'. This is more useful than saying 'p. 25 verso, bottom left illustration', because it puts the play into its context. It is also how Fiore himself refers to the plays. In this numbering system, the illustration showing the master is the first play, and all the images that follow him, up to the next master, are numbered two, three, etc. This makes it very easy to find the play referred to – simply find the right master (wearing a crown and no garter), and count from there.

Also, I'll be referring to the page numbers in the manuscript(s) in a way that may be unfamiliar to lay readers. A page of a manuscript is a 'folio', and it has two sides. The one on the right-hand side is called the 'recto', and the one on the left when you turn the page is the 'verso'. So a page reference will be something like f23r, which means 'folio 23, recto side'. Also it is worth noting that the pagination in general use, and which I am using here, is different to that employed by the Getty Museum; because the first page has a '3' written into the corner, we number the treatise from page three onwards; the Getty numbers the pages from the first extant page. Pagination is a little different in the Pisani-Dossi manuscript: Novati used 'carta' (Latin for folio), and A and B for recto and verso, so a page reference for that MS would be for example 'carta 22B'.

THE MARTIAL CONTEXT

We must also establish what kind of combat situation Fiore's art is intended to work for. It is very important because the martial context determines what works: what counts as 'winning the fight'. Consider the difference between warfare, where it's perfectly okay to shoot people from far away, and an MMA championship bout, where no weapons are allowed and you're not supposed to kill your opponent. Snipers and MMA champions are both very highly trained martial artists. Their training will have some common components, such as fitness and strength, but will otherwise be completely different.

The primary context that Fiore discusses in his introduction is fighting in the lists (*in sbarra*). This was a public display of martial prowess, fought one-on-one, usually in armour, and with a variety of knightly weapons. It includes everything from a judicial duel, to a feat of arms, a joust or a tournament. The key elements are that it is pre-arranged, between social equals, with agreed weapons. It may be fought to the death, or for a prize, or simply for honour.

Fiore also is careful to mention that other masters, jealous of his client list and fame, forced him to fight five times in just an arming jacket and gloves, with sharp swords. He says that this is more dangerous than fighting in the lists, because if you miss a single parry, you will probably die, but in the lists you can be hit many times and still win. He also explicitly states that most people survive fighting in the lists because the loser may be held for ransom. This may explain why many of Fiore's techniques such as armlocks are non-lethal, and intended to force the opponent to yield.

As the introduction segues into a description of his wrestling, he mentions that wrestling can be for fun, or in earnest (to the death), and that he is most concerned with the latter.

From these statements and the overall content of the book, it seems that the martial contexts of Fiore's art are primarily single combat (one on one), in a prearranged scenario. This is not necessarily applicable to warfare, dealing with ambushes, or working in a formation. It is also probably not very applicable to friendly tournament fencing (in this century or in his).

This makes sense historically, because in this period it was generally assumed that prowess in the lists equated to prowess in the field, and when there were no actual battles being fought, the lists gave members the knightly class their best chance of being noticed and promoted: to gain renown.

There are many excellent books on combat in the lists, such as Steven Muhlberger's *Royal Jousts at the End of the Fourteenth Century, Formal Combats in the Fourteenth Century*, or his *Deeds of Arms*. Noel Fallows's *Jousting in Medieval and Renaissance Iberia* is outstanding on the context and equipment of the joust. No reading list regarding fourteenth century single combat would be complete without Richard W. Kaeuper and Elspeth Kennedy's *The Book of Chivalry of Geoffroi de Charny: Text, Context, and Translation*.

AND WHY SHOULD YOU LISTEN TO ME?

It's a fair question. Who am I that you should bother reading my opinion? I began working on historical fencing sources in 1993, which led to co-founding the Dawn Duellists' Society in 1994, the same year that I first came across a very poor photocopy of the Pisani-Dossi manuscript. After seven years of running the Dawn Duellists Society, I moved to Helsinki, Finland, and opened the School of European Swordsmanship, teaching historical martial arts full time. From the beginning (on 17 March, 2001) I've made my living researching and teaching these arts full time, with *Il Fior di Battaglia* as my primary source. I have many thousands of hours of research, training, and teaching under my belt, and my interpretation has been tested in the Salle, and in other environments such as competitive fencing and consulting colleagues in other martial arts. I test every interpretation with blunt swords, both fast and slow, and with sharp swords both fast and slow. At every stage I have been publishing my results, and learning from the responses I get from the historical martial arts community. This began with the publication of my first book, *The Swordsman's Companion,* in 2004, and I've produced five other books on Fiore's art so far. This is in addition to translating Vadi's *De Arte Gladiatoria Dimicandi* (published as *The Art of Sword Fighting in Earnest*), writing the definitive guide to Capoferro's rapier fencing (*The Duellist's Companion,* 2006 and 2023), and two more general works, *Swordfighting for Writers, Game Designers, and Martial Artists,* and *The Theory and Practice of Historical Martial Arts.*

In 2013 I created the Syllabus Wiki, which put the syllabi I have created (for Fiore, Capoferro, Vadi, and other sources) online in video format for free. I travel all over the world to teach seminars, so I have seen my interpretations practised by thousands of people from dozens of countries and backgrounds.

As you can see, transparency is all: I *need* people to know what my interpretations are so they can comment, criticise, agree, disagree, and in general help me improve them. In the quest for similar feedback on my academic work, I submitted three of my books to Edinburgh University for a PhD by Research Publications which they granted (after much travail), in 2018.[1]

None of this means I'm right, of course. But I certainly know the sources inside out and backwards, can work with them in their original language, can execute my interpretation at speed under pressure, and can teach others to do the same. This book will give you a solid idea regarding how I see this source, and how I interpret Fiore's wrestling plays. It's up to you to decide how correct you think I may be. If you agree with absolutely everything I say, you're probably not paying close enough attention!

---

1   You can find the full story here: https://guywindsor.net/2018/02/doctor-who/

ALL WORK AND NO PLAY:
COMPARING THE WRESTLING OF FIORE DE LIBERI TO THAT OF THE LIECHTENAUER TRADITION

BY JESSICA FINLEY

My first introduction to the art of Fiore de Liberi was in the early 2000s in Tulsa, Oklahoma. Bob Charron had been invited to teach his interpretation of Fiore's system, and as I had only recently discovered the joy of working with medieval manuscripts, I was excited to attend and learn about this master and what he had written about fighting. Up to that point, I had only taken a single seminar on Liechtenauer's system with Christian Tobler, but had been reading extensively about medieval martial arts systems, and was ready to be in the room doing physical practice with fellow enthusiasts. It has been a long time since that weekend, but my main takeaway was how clear and concise Fiore's art seemed to be when compared to the diversity of techniques I had learned in the seminar on German Longsword. Returning to Fiore after twenty years of focus on German medieval martial arts, I still find myself impressed with his organization and brevity, as well as the completeness of his instruction in the art of arms.

In the introduction to his treatise, Fiore details how we are to understand his book and use it to remember and understand his fighting art. He lets us know that he is beginning with wrestling, of which there are two types: wrestling for fun, and wrestling in earnest or for your life in mortal combat. We certainly see this division in the German arts as well, with those treatises illustrating both techniques which are clearly meant for play, and those that you cannot do to an opponent without grave injury, which should be retained for earnest situations. The German treatises seem to show a wide variety of wrestling in a diversity of contexts, from play or competition, to things useful in self defense, and even holds which are for retaining captives from the battlefield. Fiore, however, restrains himself and concentrates his efforts on the most common situations you're likely to encounter in an earnest situation. This explains the striking difference in breadth between the two systems, as the German wrestling treatises show dozens of plays, ranging from Lignitzer which has 17 plays and a counter for each (more than 34) up to Baumann which has 94 plays, whereas Fiore only has sixteen techniques total. If we were to take the effort to distill the earnest wrestling plays out of the German tradition, however, I think we would find that the numbers would become much more similar.

It is intriguing to me that Fiore decided to limit his teaching so significantly when he clearly knows the wrestling that would be used for friendly competition. After all, wrestling was a common activity for the medieval person to engage in for health and fitness. It is recommended along with such exercises as running, jumping, swimming, and the lifting and throwing of heavy stones in order to maintain a supple body and a mind free from worry.

Fiore tells us in his introduction that he is laying the book out according to the preferences of his lord to whom he dedicates the book, and I am reminded of a section of one of Talhoffer's books where he gives instruction on preparation for a duel. It seems that sometimes the medieval masters were not trying to give a comprehensive system for every use case of martial arts, but instead focused on a complete exploration of that one singular context.

After understanding the context he is preparing us for, we are advised to consider the important qualities of any opponent. Fiore suggests you should assess whether they are weaker or stronger than yourself, older or younger, and if they seem to have knowledge of wrestling. Then he tells us that we should have knowledge of holds and locks and how to defend ourselves from them. Fiore continues to expand on this idea, explaining in more detail the qualities that a person needs in order to be a good grappler, and these qualities are broadly Strength, Speed, and Knowledge. Of Knowledge, he gives us six things we should know: superior holds, breaking limbs, locks, strikes, throws, and dislocations. Of course, in order to use any of these things we know, we will need strength and speed to properly apply them.

While Fiore does not explain further how these qualities are to be used or precisely what they are for, the German traditions have a more explicit breakdown of the same idea. The 15th century wrestling master Ott tells us that wrestling needs Strength, Speed, and Skill, and that of these, speed is the best as it prevents us from being countered. Against a weaker opponent we should attack first, but against a stronger opponent we should wait and respond to him, and in the case of an equal opponent we should attack at the same time. Ott goes further to say that if we are attacking first we should use speed, if all things are equal we will need balance, but if we are responding to them we must attack vulnerable points like the joint of the knee. We cannot know for sure if Fiore would agree with Ott's advice regarding the timing of our attacks, but as we will see, his *posta* imply the same considerations; in some we should advance, and in others be patient and wait to foul their attack.

Fiore begins the physical instruction for his wrestling section with four posta or common useful positions you should adopt while wrestling. As a student of medieval mnemonic structures, his presentation of the posta strikes me as particularly clever. The first two posta have the hands separated, right hand high, and left hand low. Posta Longa (the Long Guard) has the right arm extended long and high, and Posta Di Dente Di Zenghiaro (the Boar's Tooth) has the right arm bent upward to about ninety degrees. In this way we can imagine this as a pair, one that is driving forward with the long arm, one that is driving upwards with the bent arm. The next two posta also seem paired, with both hands moving together. Posta Di Porta di Ferro (the Iron Door) is shown with both hands down and a left leg lead, whereas Posta Frontale (the Frontal Guard) has both hands up with extended arms, and the right leg leading. Porta di Ferro and Frontale highlight patience and assertiveness, whereas Longa and Dente di Zenghiaro highlight extension and retraction, after all, Fiore tells us that they counter each other, so thinking of them in these broad terms helps us find their application in more contexts.

Top Left: Longa; *Top Right*: Dente di Zenghiaro;
Bottom Left: Porta Di Ferro: *Bottom Right*: Frontale

Attacking with Frontale will force your opponent to abandon Porta di Ferro, he says, but also cautions us not to remain in Frontale but instead to move to another position. Porta di Ferro, meanwhile, is full of malice and gives us strong grips to make the opponent go to the ground. These two guards are most similar to the types of entry positions we see in German manuscripts, and the advice is similar.

Left: Königsegg-Aulendorf copy of Talhoffer 144601459;
Right: Fabian von Auerswald, 1537

Fabian von Auerswald admonishes us in his 1537 treatise: "First, see if your opponent goes high or low. If he goes high, then you shouldn't worry and perform the plays that you can freely perform on him. If he goes low, then you have to pay good attention to him." This advice certainly seems to align with Fiore's warnings about the pain that the Iron Door can give to whomever comes against it!

Looking a little deeper into how we are to use these guards, we are told to attack with *Frontale* in order to gain our grips from which we will wrestle. However, Fiore doesn't seem to spend any time on these grips. What are we intended to grasp? The German wrestling masters spend very little time on guards for wrestling, not even naming them, but do spend quite a bit of time on the grips. These are broadly broken into grips at the arms, and grips at the body. These holds can be reciprocal, where no innate advantage is given to either party, or can be unequal to work to one's own strengths. But before any grip can be gained, there is the fighting for advantage, which is what Fiore seems to be focused on with his posta.

Left: Grip at the body; *Right*: Grip at the Arms

Fiore lists for us the places we should attack our opponents, either to enact true damage or to cause enough pain to gain compliance or to create a moment to exploit. These are striking to the eyes, the nose, the throat, or the flanks. Again, Auerswald has similar advice, saying "one should pay diligent attention to whether one comes with outstretched limbs or crooked. The one who comes to another with extended limbs is easiest to bring to weakness and thereafter subdue, particularly when one knows to grasp the weak points or joints of the body: the hands and feet, whichever part of the body is closest; thereafter also the entire body, the neck, the genitals, and both places, behind or under the ears." Reaching out with *Longa* or *-Frontale* gives the advantage of length and aggression, but it is those short patient *posta* who will strike us in the places of pain.

Understanding these foundational principles, we can move into the first play of wrestling, which is an exemplar of how Fiore structures his whole treatise, and a beautiful little microcosm of the art of wrestling. Though he doesn't tell us which posta the players have begun in, nor precisely who initiated the encounter, we can imagine that both players have begun in *Porta di Ferro* and the one on the left begins to attempt to grapple moving into *Frontale*. The master then drives in, stepping outside with the right foot with the right hand inside and under the left arm of the opponent, and blocking out their right arm with the left hand at the inside of the elbow. From here, he immediately bends his right arm to *Dente Di Zenghiaro*. This position is an inflection point, a place from which he can test the opponent and make a choice about how he will continue with a throw, break, or dislocation.

Though German masters don't spend time discussing posta, they do talk a lot about these moments where one must make a decision about how to continue the attack. As Ott says, we must pay attention to the balance, that is taking the myriad of sensory inputs we are receiving from our opponent and comparing them to our own impetus. For instance, are they pushing against us, or yielding? Are they softening up or digging in their heels? Are they moving to counter us or freezing up in indecision? We must use *Fühlen*, or feeling, to weigh all of these things, and to moderate our attack accordingly. Auerswald describes a similar position to that of Fiore's first master, calling it "winding off short before the hand in order to test how he will react to a hold". Once you have made the test, you should swiftly and immediately continue the attack according to the principles Fiore outlines.

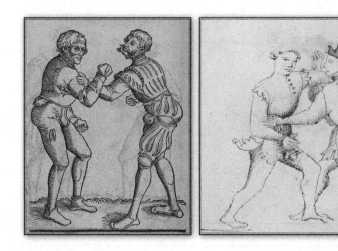

Left: Auerswald's Winding Off; *Right*: Fiore's First Master

Moving forward with the play, if the opponent doesn't make a reaction to the adopting of the Boar's Tooth in the test, Fiore advises us to immediately perform the second play, turning him and throwing him to the ground or dislocating his arm. This throw will put the opponent on their face and this style of forward throw occurs frequently in the German manuscripts. Andres Lignitzer details the throw this way: "Strike his left hand from underneath with your right hand so that you have it on your right shoulder. Spring with your right leg in front of his left leg and wrap your right arm from the outside around his left arm. Help your right arm with your left hand and turn yourself away from him to your left side." Paulus Kal shows the same thing in his manuscript, as you can see below.

Left: Kal prepping to swing away and through his opponent;
Right: Fiore having turned and the oppenent about to fall down.

Forward throws using the hand, elbow, or shoulder to leverage the opponent are extremely common in the German medieval wrestling corpus, and are depicted from a wide variety of grips and set-ups. In my experience, this particular version (locking up the upper arm and elbow) is incredibly versatile. It will work in and out of armor, on horseback, and when armed. It would seem that Fiore felt this particular version had the most usefulness in the contexts he was imagining as well.

It is interesting that the German texts tend to advise stepping in front of the opponent's foot with the right foot, however Fiore steps to the outside. In my mind, this shows a continued caginess on the part of Fiore's advice. Stepping in front more guarantees that the opponent's balance will be broken and the throw is likely to happen, and for the German system who want their techniques to work in play as well as in earnest, this makes sense. In competition, the win happens at the throw. Fiore, however, is as happy for this to make a dislocation or an arm break for his context, so rather than overcommit to benefit the single outcome, he hedges his bets and relies on his continued ability to press the attack if he is foiled.

In order to prevent this technique, the opponent must get their left arm free from the shoulder or neck to then be able to apply their own defenses. Fiore doesn't give us specifics about how this might be done, but the counter that Lignitzer describes can give us insight into what Fiore may have intended: "When someone does this to you and pushes your left arm on his neck, slip your left arm over his head and in front of his chest. Grab his left arm with your left hand and reach behind his right knee from the outside with your right hand. Lift his knee joint up and push him down to your left side with your left arm. This is how you throw him on his back." This counter only works if the attacker has stepped in front of you. Fiore has protected us against it by having us step to the outside to begin with, but the arm slipping over the head and blocking low to their left arm is still a reasonable defense and gives us the position that Fiore shows for his third play.

Left: Auerswald with a less generous low grip;
Right: Fiore's Third play, moving from the second.

The third play continues from the second, if the opponent has slipped the arm. Fiore tells us that with this play he will send the opponent to the ground on his back, and Lignitzer's next play advises the same. He says, "Go with your right arm from the outside over his left arm in front of his chest and grab him by his right shoulder. Spring with your right leg behind his left leg and grab him behind his left knee from the inside with your left hand. Throw him on your right side." We can absolutely see a continuity of techniques that are shared between the German wrestling systems and the concepts that Fiore is teaching with his foundational plays.

It is beyond the scope of this article to continue on in this manner, detailing the similarities and differences between the medieval wrestling techniques highlighted in various treatises. While students of the German systems might at first find Fiore's teaching through *posta* to be confounding, the techniques themselves aren't unique to him. German medieval fighting texts tend to present opposites in proximity to each other in order to highlight their unique qualities. Fiore tends to show the flow from a single position to its logical conclusion. The difference isn't so much in the actions themselves, but how we are to understand them and their relationship to other actions.

It is clear to me that Fiore was well versed in wrestling and in the likely responses to certain stimuli when it is given by an opponent, but it seems to me that he expected his students and the patron for whom he was writing to have a solid understanding of these things as well. He doesn't feel a need to elaborate on the grips, the entries, or why one might choose a particular posta over another. Because he is only showing a small portion of the art of wrestling, it would benefit the student of Fiore to broaden their reading and study the friendly and competitive context taught in the German system, in order that they might better understand Fiore's selections and what that means about his broader choices in his armed instruction.

FIORE'S INTRODUCTION

FIORE'S INTRODUCTION, PART ONE

This introduces us to Fiore, gives some background into his life, his students, their many victories, and dedicates the book, with the most fulsome and hard to translate praise, to Niccolo d'Este, Marquis of Ferrara.

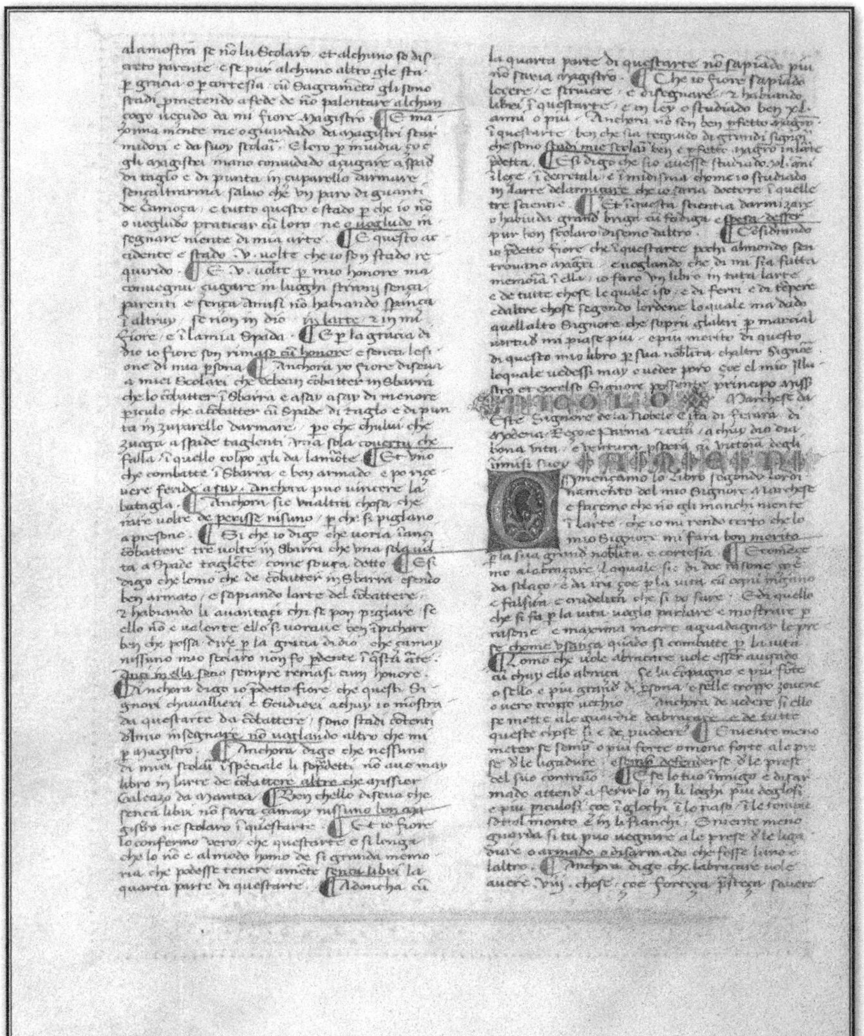

Fior Furlan de Civida d'ostria che fo di misser Benedetto de la nobel casada de li liberi da Premeriias de la diiocesi dello Patriarchado de Aquilegia in sua zoventu volse inprender ad armizare & arte de combatter in Sbarra, De lanza, Azza, Spada e daga, e de abrazare a pe e acavallo, in Arme e senca Arme.

Fior Furlan from Civida[le] in Ostria, son of the late sir Benedetto, of the noble house of the Liberi from Premariacco in the diocese of the Patriarchy of Aquileia, in his youth wished to understand armoured combat (armizare) and the art of combat in the lists, with the lance, axe, sword and dagger, and wrestling, on foot and on horseback, in armour and without armour.

Anchora volse savere tempere di ferri. E fatezze de zaschuna Arma tanto a defendere quanto ad offendere, e maxima mente chose de combatter ad oltranza.

Also he wished to know the temper of irons. And skill at any weapon, as much to defend as to attack, and especially things to do with combat to the death.

Anchora altre chose meraveglose e oculte le quale a pochi homini del mondo sono palese. E sono chose verissime e de grandissima offesa, e de grande deffesa, e chose che non se po fallare tanto sono lizie a fare. La quale arte e magisterio ch'e ditto di sopra.

Also other marvellous and secret things, which are known to few men in the world. And they are very true things, of maximum offence, and great defence, and things that cannot fail because they are so easy to do. This art and mastery that is spoken of above.

E lo ditto Fiore si a imprese le ditte chose da molti Magistri todeschi e di molti Italiani in piu provincie & in molte citadi cum grandissima e cum grande spese.

And the said Fiore did learn the said things from many German Masters and from many Italians, in many provinces and in many cities, with the greatest [? Probably 'effort' is missing] and with great expense.

E per la gracia di dio, da tanti Magistri e Scolari. E in corte di grandi Signori, principi, ducha Marchesi e conti, chavalieri e Schudieri in tanto a impresa questa Arte. Che lo ditto Fiore a stado piu e piu volte richesto da molti Signori e chavallieri e schudieri per imprender del ditto Fiore si fatta arte d'armizare e de combatter in Sbarra a oltranza la quale arte ello a monstrada a piu sori italiani e todeschi & altri grandi Signori che ano debudo combattere in Sbarra. E Ancho ad infiniti che non ano debudo combattere. E de alguni che [column break] *sono stadi miei Scolari che ano debudo combatter in Sbarra. De quali alchuni qui ne faro nome e memoria.*

Primo de loro si fo el nobele e gaglardo chavaliero Misser piero del Verde el quale debea conbattere cum Missier piero dela corona i quali forono ambi doii todeschi. E la Batagla debea esser a Perosa.

Anchora a lo valoroso chavalliero Missier Nicolo Wrizilino thodesco che debea combatter cum nicolo Inghileso. Lo campo fo dado ad Imola.

And by the grace of God, from so many Masters and Scholars. And in the courts of great lords, princes, dukes, marquises and counts, knights and squires, just to learn this art. That the said Fiore has been more and more times requested by many lords, knights, and squires to teach the said Fiore who does the art of armed combat and of combat in the lists to the death, the which art he has shown to many Italians and Germans, and other great lords that have had to fight in the lists. And also to countless [others] who have not had to fight. And of some who [column break] have been my scholars that have had to fight in the lists.[1] Of these some I will name and remember here.

First of them is the noble and strong knight Sir Piero del Verde, who had to fight with Sir Piero dela Corona in which [fight] both were German. And the combat had to be a Perugia.

Also the valiant German knight Sir Nicolo Wrizilino[2] that had to fight with Nicolo the English. The field was held at Imola.

---

1 Note that Fiore switches from the third person to first person here.
2 Leoni identifies this knight as von Urslingen.

Anchora al notabele valoroso, e gaglardo chavalliero Misse Galeazo di Captani da Grimello chiamado da Mantoa che debea combattere cum lo valoroso chavalliero Missier Buzichardo de Fraza, lo campo fo a Padoa.

Also the notable, valiant, and strong knight Sir Galeazo di Captani of Grimello, called da Mantoa, who had to fight with the valiant knight Sir Boucicault of France, the field was at Padua.[3]

Anchora al valoroso schudiero Lancilotto da Becharia de Pavia, el quale se ·vi· punti de lanza a ferri moladi a chavallo, contra lo valente cavalliero Missier Baldassaro todescho I quali ad Iimola debea combatter in Sbarra.

Also the valiant squire Lancilotto of Becharia from Pavia, the which had six thrusts of the sharp-tipped lance on horseback, against the valiant knight Sir Baldassaro the German, who at Imola had to fight in the lists.

Anchora al valoroso Schudiero zoanino da Baiio da Milano che fe in Pavia in lo castello contra lo valente Schudiero Sram todesco tre punti di lanza a ferri moladi achavallo. E poii fe a pe tre colpi de Azza, e tre colpi de Spada e tre colpi di daga in presenza del Nobilissimo principo e Signore Missier lo Ducha da Milano e de Madona la duchessa, e d'altri infiniti Signori e donne.

Also the valiant squire Zoanino of Baio from Milan, who made in Pavia in the castle against the bold squire Sram the German, three thrusts of the sharp-tipped lance on horseback. And then made on foot three blows of the axe, and three blows of the sword, and three blows of the dagger, in the presence of the most noble Prince and Lord the Duke of Milan and my Lady the Duchess, and of innumerable other lords and ladies.

---

3   Both Galeazzo da Mantoa and Jean le Maingre (known as Boucicault) were famous knights of this period, and in fact fought twice at Padua, the first time on August 22nd 1395, giving us the earliest possible date for this manuscript.

Anchora al cauteloso chavalliero Missier Azzo da Castell Barcho che debea una volta combatter cum zuanne di Ordelaffi. E un'altra volta cum lo valente e bon chavalliero Missier Jacomo da Boson, e'l campo debea esser al piasere delo Signore ducha di Milano.

Also the cautious knight sir Azzo da Castell Barcho, that one time had to fight with Zuanne di Ordelaffi. And one other time with the bold and good knight Sir Jacomo da Boson, and the field had to be at the pleasure of the Lord Duke of Milan.

Di questi e d'altri i quali io Fiore o magistradi, io son molto contento per che io son stado ben rimunerato & o habudo l'onore e l'amore di miei Scolari e di parenti loro. Digo Anchora che questa arte io l'o mostrada sempre oculta mente si che non gle sta presente alchuno [page break: F1r to F1v] a la mostra se non lu Scolaro, et alchuno so discreto parente e se pur alchuno altro gl'e sta per gracia o per cortesia, cum Sagramento gli sono stadi prometendo a fede de non palesare alchun zogo vezudo da mi Fiore Magistro.

Of these and of others of whom I Fiore was their teacher, I am very happy because I have been well paid and have had the honour and love of my scholars and of their families. I say again that these arts I have shown often in secret so that only the scholar, and some discreet members of their family, are present. And if any others are there by grace or courtesy, with a sacred promise they swear to not show any play they have seen from me, Fiore the Master.

E mazorma mente me o guardado da Magistri scarmidori e da suoii scolari. E loro per invidia zoe gli Magistri m'ano convidado a zugare a spade di taglo e di punta in zuparello d'armare senz'altr'arma salvo che un paro di guanti de Camoza, e tutto questo è stado per che io non o vogludo praticar cum loro, ne o vogludo insegnare niente di mia arte.

And especially I have been careful of fencing masters and their scholars. And they through envy thus these masters have challenged me to play with swords with sharp edges and points, in an arming jacket and without other armour except a pair of chamois gloves, and all this has been because I did not want to practice with them, nor have wanted to teach them anything of my art.

E questo accidente e stado ·V· volte che io son stado requirido. E ·V· volte per mio honore m'a convegnu zugare in luoghi stranii senza parenti e senza Amisi non habiando speranza in altruii, se non in dio, in l'arte, & in mi Fiore, e in la mia Spada. E per la gracia di dio io Fiore son rimaso cum honore e senca lesione di mia persona.

And it has occurred five times, that I have been so required. And five times by my honour I have met to play, in foreign places without family and without my friends, having no hope in others, except in God, in the art, and in myself Fiore, and in my sword. And by the grace of God I Fiore have remained with honour and without injury in my body.

Anchora iio Fiore diseva a miei Scolari che debean combatter in Sbarra che lo combatter in Sbarra a asaii asaii di menore periculo che a combatter cum Spade di taglo e di punta in zuparello d'armare, pero che chului che zuoga a spade taglenti, una sola coverta che falla, in quello colpo gli da la morte.

Also I, Fiore, tell my scholars that have to fight in the lists that the combat in the lists is so, so, much less dangerous than the fight with swords of sharp edges and points in an arming jacket, because for those that play with sharp swords, a single parry that fails, that blow gives death.

*Et uno che combatte in Sbarra e
ben armado e po rizevere feride
asaii. Anchora puo vincere la
bataglia. Anchora si'e un'altra
chosa che rare volte de perisse
nisuno, per che si piglano a
presone. Si che io digo che voria
inanci combattere tre volte in
Sbarra che una sola volta a Spade
taglente, come sovra detto.*

*E si digo che l'omo che de
combatter in Sbarra, esendo ben
armato, e sapiando l'arte del
combattere, & habiando li avantazi
che se pon piglare, se ello non e
valente ello si vorave ben impichare
ben che possa dire per la gratia di
dio, che zamaii nissuno mio scolaro
non fo perdente in questa arte.
Anci in ella sono sempre remasi
cum honore.*

*Anchora digo io predetto Fiore che
questi Signori chavallieri e Scudieri
achuii io monstrada quest'arte da
combattere, sono stadi contenti
del'mio insegnare non voglando
altro che mi per magistro.*

And one that fights in the lists is
well armoured and can recieve
many blows thus. And can also win
the fight. Also there is another
thing, that it is very unusual that
anyone dies, because they are taken
for ransom. This is why I say I
would rather fight three times in
the lists than one single time with
sharp swords, as I said above.

And so I say that the man who
fights in the lists, being well
armoured, and knowing the art of
combat, and the advantages that he
can grab, if he is not bold he could
just as well hang himself, but I can
say by the grace of God, that not
one of my scholars has been lost in
this art. And in [the art] have
always kept their honour.

Also I say that I, the aforesaid
Fiore, that these lords, knights, and
squires to whom I have shown this
art of combat, have been happy
with my teaching, not want anyone
other than me for their teacher.

Anchora digo che nessuno di miei scolari in speciale li sopradetti non ave maii libro in l'arte de combattere altre che Misser Galeazo da Mantoa. Ben ch'ello diseva che senza libri non sara zamaii nissuno bon Magistro ne scolaro in quest'arte. E io Fiore lo confermo vero, che quest'arte e si longa che lo non e al modo homo de si granda memoria che podesse tenere a'mente senca libri la quarta parte di quest'arte. Adoncha cum [column break] la quarta parte di quest'arte non sapiando più non saria magistro.

Also I say that not one of my scholars, especially the ones named above have had any books on the art of combat, other than Sir Galeazzo da Mantoa. Who avers that without books, none can ever become a good master nor scholar in this art. And I, Fiore, confirm this as true, that this art is so long that no man has so great a memory that he could hold in mind without books a quarter of this art. And even with that quarter of this art without knowing more could not be a master.

Che io Fiore sapiando legere, e scrivere, e disegnare, & habiando libri in quest'arte, e in leii o studiado ben XL. anni o più, Anchora non son ben perfetto Magistro in quest'arte, ben che sia tegnudo di grandi signori che sono stadi mie scolari ben e perfetto Magistro in l'arte predetta. E si digo che s'io avesse studiado ·xl· anni in lege, in decretali, e in midisina chome i'o studiado in l'arte del'armizare che io saria doctore in quelle tre scientie. Et in questa scientia d'armizare o habiuda grande briga cum fadiga e spesa d'esser pur bon scolaro, disemo d'altro.

That I, Fiore, knowing how to read, and write, and draw, and having books on this art, and having read and studied well for 40 years or more, even so I am not a complete master in this arte, though I have been held by great lords that have been my students as a good and complete master in the aforesaid art. And if I say that I have studied 40 years in law, in canon law, and in medicine, as I have studied in the art of arms, I would have been a doctor in these three subjects. And in this subject of the art of arms I have taken great pains, effort, and expense to be a good scholar, let's talk about something else.

Considerando io predetto Fiore che in quest'arte pochi almondo sen trovano Magistri, e voglando che di mi sia fatta memoria in ella, io faro un libro in tuta l'arte e de tutte chose le quale i'so, e di ferri e di tempere e'd'altre chose segondo l'ordene lo quale m'a dado quell'alto Signore che sopra gl'altri per marcial virtude mi piase piu, e piu merito di questo di questo mio libro per sua nobilità ch'altro Signore loquale vedessi maii e veder poro zoe el mio illustro et excelso Signore possente principo Misser NICOLO Marchese da Este, Signore de la Nobele Cita di Ferara, di Modenam, Eezo, Parma &cetera, a chuy dio dia bona vita, e ventura prospera cum victoria degli inimisi suoii AMEN

I, the aforesaid Fiore, considering than in this art there are few masters to be found in the world, and wishing to be remembered in it [the art], I am making a book about the whole art, and about all the things in it, and of iron and of temper and of the other things, by order of the one that has given the high lord that is above the others by his martial virtue, who pleases me the most, and who most deserves this, this my book, by his nobility, greater than that of the other lords I have seen or will see, thus, my illustrious and exalted lord the potent prince sir Nicolo marquis of Este, lord of the noble city of Ferrara, of Modena, Reggio, Parma, etcetera, and whom God give a good life, and prosperous fortunes, with victory over his enemies, Amen.

Part Two: Fiore's Introduction to the Treatise Itself

This explains how the book is supposed to work, such as describing the crown and garter conventions, and introduces us to wrestling in particular.

COmenzamo lo Libro segondo l'ordinamento del mio Signore Marchese e fazemo che non gli manchi niente in l'arte, che io mi rendo certo che lo mio Signore mi fara bon merito per la sua grande nobilita e cortesia. E comenzemo a l'abrazare, Loquale si'e di doe rasone zoe da solazo, e da ira zoe per la vita cum ogni inganno e falsita e crudelita che si po fare. E di quello che si fa per la vita voglo parlare e mostrare per rasone, e maxima mente a guadagnar le prese chom'e usanza quando si combatte per la vita.

L'omo che vole abracare vole esser avisado cum chuy ello abraza, se lu compagno e piu forte o s'ello e piu grande di persona e s'elle troppo zovene o vero troppo vechio. Anchora de vedere si ello se mette ale guardie d'abrazare, e de tutte queste chose si e de prevedere.

Beginning the book according to the instruction of my lord Marquis, and making it so that nothing in the art is left out, that I will make sure that my lord will be please with me, through his great nobility and courtesy. And we begin with wrestling, the which is of two kinds, thus, of leisure, and of anger, thus, for your life with every trick and deception and cruelty that you can do. And of that which is done for your life, I wish to speak and show with reason, and especially to gain the grips as are used when in a fight for your life.

The man who wants to wrestle must be familiar with the one they will wrestle, if the companion is stronger, or is bigger in their body, or is too young, or too old. Also see if he places himself in the guards of wrestling, and all these things are to be seen in advance.

E niente meno meter se sempre o piu forte o meno forte ale prese de le ligadure, e sempre defenderse dele prese del suo contrario.

And nothing less than always put on, whether stronger or less strong at the grips of the binds, and always defend yourself from the grips of his counter.

E se lo tuo inimigo e disarmado attende a ferirlo in li loghi più doglosi e piu periculosi zoe in gl'ochi in lo naso, in le tempie sotto'l mento e in li fianchi. E niente meno guarda si tu puo vegnire a le prese de le ligadure o armado o disarmado che fosse l'uno e l'altro.

And if your enemy is unarmoured, pay attention to strike in the places more painful and more dangerous, thus in the eyes, in the nose, in the temples, under the chin, and in the flanks. And nothing less watch that you can come to the grips from the binds, whether armoured or unarmoured, that you can do one and the other.

Anchora digo che l'abrazare vole avere ·viii· chose zoe Forteza presteza savere [page break: F2v] zoe saver prese avantizade, savere far roture zoe romper brazi e gambe, saver ligadure zoe Ligar brazi per modo che'l homo non habia piu defesa ne se possa partire in sua liberta, Saver ferire in luogo piu periculoso. Anchora save mettere uno in terra senza periculo di si instesso. Anchora saver dislogar brazi e gambi per diversi modi. Le quale tutte chose scriviro e poro depinte in questo libro de grado in grado chomo vole l'arte.

Also I say that wrestling wants to have eight things, thus, Strength, speed, knowledge of advantageous grips, knowledge of how to make breaks (thus, breaking arms and legs), knowledge of binds (thus binding the arms in such a way that the man cannot defend himself nor can he gain his freedom), knowledge of striking in the places most dangerous. Also knowledge of putting one on the ground without danger to himself. Also knowledge of dislocating arms and legs in various ways. I will write about all these things, and will show them in this book step by step as the art requires.

Noi avemo ditto zo che vole l'abrazare, ora disemo delle guardie d'abrazare. Le guardie del abrazare si po fare per diversi modi. & un modo e miglore del altro. Ma queste ·iiii· guardie so le miglore in arme e senz'arme, avegna dio che le guardie non a stabilita per le prese subite che se fano.

We have spoken about what wrestling requires, now lets discuss the guards of wrestling. The guards of wrestling can be done in various ways. And one is better than the other. But these four guards are the best in armour and out of armour. I advise you that the guards are not stable, because of the grips that they immediately do.

E lli primi quatro Magistri che vederiti cum le corone in testa, per quegli si mostra le guardie del Abrazare, zoè Posta longa, e dente di cengiaro le quali fano una in contra l'altra, e poii fano porta di ferro e posta frontale l'una in contra l'altra. E queste ·iiii·guardie pon fare tutte chose che denanzi sono ditte del abrazare in arme e senz'arme zoè prese e ligadure e roture &cetera

And the first four masters that you will see with crowns on their heads, by these are shown the guards of wrestling, thus long guard, and boar's tooth, the which are done one against the other, and then are the iron door and frontal guard, one against the other. And these four guards can do all the things that are said before about wrestling, in armour and out of armour, thus, grips and binds and breaks etcetera.

Mo bisogna fare per modo che le guardie sen cognosca delli Magistri Zugadori, e lli scolari da zugadori, e lli zugadori de Magistri, e lo remedio del contrario, ben che sempre lo contrario e posto dredo al remedio, e tal volta dredo lo remedio o dredo tutti li soii zogi. e di questo faremo chiareza.

We must do it this way, that the guards are distinguished from the Masters [and] Players, and the scholars from the players, and the players from the masters, and the remedy from the counter, always the counter is placed after the remedy, and sometimes [immediately] after the remedy or after all of its plays, and this we will make clear.

Noi disemo che a cognosser le guardie overo poste e lizera chosa, prima che le guardie ano lor arme in mano l'una contra l'altra, e non si tochano l'una cum l'altra. E stano avisade e ferme una contra l'altra per vedere zo che lo compagno vol fare. E queste sono chiamade poste overo guardie overo primi Magistri de la Bataglia. E questi portano corona in testa, per che sono poste in logo e per modo di fare grande defesa cum esso tale aspetare. E sono principio di quell'arte zoe di quell'arte de l'arma cum la quale li ditti Magistri stano in guardia.

We see that to know the guards, or poste, is an easy thing. First that the guards have their weapon in hand one against the other, and they do not touch each other. And they stand wary and still, one against the other, to see what the companion wants to do. And these are called positions, or guards, or first Masters of the Battle. And these wear a crown on their heads, because they are placed in a way to make great defence, which they wait for. And they are the beginning of this art, thus in the art of the weapon with which the said Masters stand on guard.

E tanto e a dire posta che guardia. E guardia e tanto a dire che l'omo se guarda, e se defende cum quella, de le feride del suo inimigo. E tanto e a dire posta che modo de apostar lo inimigo suo per offenderlo senza periculo di se instesso.

And it is as much to say 'guard' as 'ward'. And guards are as much to say that the man guards, and defends with it, from the attacks of his enemy. And it is as much to say that "posta" is the way of positioning himself, to offend his enemy without danger to himself.[1]

---

1   Note: I ue 'guard' for 'posta' and for 'guardia', because, as Fiore says, they are the same thing. To translate this sentence I have chosen 'guard' and 'ward', because they derive from the same root, and are essentially the same word. Their range of meanings are different but overlap to a considerable degree.

L'altro Magistro che seguita le ·iiii· guardie, vene ad ensire de le guardie, e si vene a defenderse d'un altro zugadore cum gli colpi che esseno de le ·iiii· guardie che sono denanzi. E questo Magistro porta anchora corona, e si e chiamado secondo Magistro. Anchora si e chiamado Magistro remedio per che ello fa lo remedio che non gli siano dade de le feride overo che non gli sia fatta inzuria in quell'arte che sono le ditte poste overo guardie.

The other Master that follows the four guards, goes to show what follows from the guards, and goes to defend himself against another player with the blows that come from the four guards that are before. And this master also wears a crown, and is called 'second Master'. Also he is called 'remedy Master', because he makes the remedy so that he will not be hit by the attack, or that he will not be injured in this art, that are the said guards or wards.

E questo segondo zoe rimedio si a alguni zugadori sotto di si i'quali zugano quelli zogi che poria zugare lo Magistro ch'e d'avanti zoe lo rimedio piglando quella coverta overo presa che fa lo ditto rimedio. E questi zugadori portarano una divisa sotto lo zinochio. E sarano questi zugadori tutti li zoghi de lo rimedio in fin tanto che si trovara un altro Magistro che fara lu contrario de lo rimedio e di tutti suoi zugadori.

And this second or remedy has some players players below which play the plays that can be played by the master that is before, so, the remedy grabbing that cover or grip that makes the said remedy. And these players will wear a device[2] [in this case, a garter] under the knee. And these players will do all the plays of the remedy, up to the point that another master is found, that makes the counter to the remedy and to all his players.

---

2   In this treatise, a garter. The Italian word *divisa* means "device". Garter would be *giarrettiera*, or *gancio*.

E perzo ch'ello fa contra lo rimedio e contra soii zugadori, ello portera la divisa de lo Magistro rimedio e de soi zugadori zoe la corona in testa e la divisa sotto lo zinochio, E questo Re e chiamado Magistro terzo, e de chiamado contrario per che sara contra gl'altri Magistri e contra a soi zogi.

And because he makes the counter to the remedy and the counter to his players, he will wear the device of the remedy Master and of his players, thus the crown on his head and the device under his knee. And this King is called the third master, and is called 'counter', because he will be counter to the other masters and counter to their plays.

Anchora digo che in alchuni loghi in l'arte si trova lo quarto magistro zoe Re che fa contra lo terzo Re, zoe lo contrario delo rimedio. E questo Re, e lo magistro quarto chiamado Magistro quarto. E de chiamado contra contrario, Ben che pochi zogi passano lo terzo Magistro in l'arte. E si piu s'in fano, se fa cum periculo. E basta di questo ditto.

Also I say that in some places in the art is found the fourth master, thus the King that makes the counter to the third King, thus the counter to the remedy. And this King is the fourth master called "fourth master". And he is called "counter-counter", though few plays go beyond the third master in the art. And if one goes so far, one goes with danger. And enough of this, I say.

Como noii averno parlado qui dinanzi de le guardie d'abrazare, e del Segondo Magistro zoe del rimedio e deli soi Zugadori, E del terzo Magistro contrario al segondo Magistro & a soii zugadori, E del quarto Magistro ch'e chiamado contra contrario, chosi come questi Magistri e zugadori ano a rezere l'arte d'abrazare in arme e senza arme, chosi ano questi magistri e zugadori a rezere l'arte de la lanza cum le lanze e loro guardie Magistri e zugadori. Et per lo simile cum la Azza, e cum la spada d'una mano e de doii mani. E per lo simile cum la daga.

As we have spoken above about the guards of abrazare, and of the Second Master or remedy, and of his Players, and of the third Master the counter to the second master and his players, and of the fourth master that is called counter-counter, so as these Masters and players are the basis of the art of wrestling in armour and without armour, so these masters and players are the basis of the art of the lance, with the lances and their guards, Masters, and players. And in the same way with the Axe, and with the sword in one hand and in two hands. And in the same way with the dagger.

Si che per efetto questi magistri e zugadori detti dinanzi cum le insegne loro e divise ano a rezere tutta l'arte d'armizare a pe e dacavallo in arme e senz'arme. Segondo ch'elli fano in lo zogho del abrazare.

So in effect these masters and players spoken of before with their insignia and devices are the basis of the whole art of arms on foot and on horseback, in armour and without armour, just as they are in the plays of wrestling.

E queste s'intende solamente pero che chosi bisogna esser guardie e Magistri in le altre arte e rimedii e contrarii come in l'arte de Abrazare azo che lo libro si possa licera mente intendere. Ben che le Rubriche e le figure, e li zoghi mostrarano tutta l'arte si bene che tutta la si pora intendere. Ora atendemo ale figure depinte e a lor zoghi & a loro parole le quale ne mostrara la veritade.

And this is just to say that there needs to be guards and masters in the other arts, and remedies and counters as in the art of wrestling, so that the book can be easily understood. Just as the red text and the figures, and the plays will show the whole art so well that all can be understood. Now we pay attention to the drawn figures, and to their plays, and to their words, which will show the truth of this.

LESSONS FOR ABRAZARE, FROM FIORE'S INTRODUCTION

The Crown and Garter
Symbols

One of Fiore's greatest strokes of genius is the way he makes it absolutely clear which figure is doing the described play, in every illustration. He does this with his crown and garter convention. As he described in the introduction, and as he executed entirely consistently throughout the manuscripts (for which his name be forever praised), he has a system for indicating not only who is doing the play, but also where that action fits in the overall hierarchy of actions. In the manuscripts you will see people with:

- A crown, on their own.
- A crown, in contact with another person.
- A garter, always in contact with another person.
- A crown and a garter, always in contact with another person.
- No insignia at all.

The figures that begin each section are shown standing in guard, and wear a crown to indicate their masterly status. They are the "first masters".

Following them are one or more "remedy masters" (also called the "second masters"), who illustrate a defence against an attack. Following each of them in turn are their scholars, identified by a garter, who execute the techniques that follow the previous master's remedy.

After a scholar or master may come a "counter-remedy master" (the "third master"), wearing a crown and a garter, who illustrates the counter to the remedy master, or to one of the remedy master's scholars.

Occasionally, there is a fourth master, who may be called the "counter-counter-remedy master", who wears the crown and garter too.

Fiore specifies that most sequences don't get beyond the third master (i.e. the attack is met by the remedy, which the attacker counters), and it is perilous (perhaps because it is insecure) to go beyond three or four. The players (*zugadore*) or companions (*compagni*) are the "losers" in every play, and have no insignia.

This visual convention is unique to Fiore as far as we know, and makes it easy to be sure who is supposed to win from any illustrated position, and what stage of the fight (principle or guard; defence; counter to the defence; counter to the counter) is being shown. When reading the treatise, you can immediately identify who is winning in a given picture by his bling – the most bling wins!

THE EIGHT THINGS

As we saw, Fiore wrote in his introduction:

"Also I say that wrestling wants to have eight things, thus, Strength, speed, knowledge of advantageous grips, knowledge of how to make breaks (thus, breaking arms and legs), knowledge of binds (thus binding the arms in such a way that the man cannot defend himself nor can he gain his freedom), knowledge of striking in the places most dangerous. Also knowledge of putting one on the ground without danger to himself. Also knowledge of dislocating arms and legs in various ways. I will write about all these things, and will show them in this book step by step as the art requires."

So, the "eight things" are:

1. Strength
2. Speed
3. Knowledge of advantageous grips
4. Knowledge of breaking arms and legs
5. Knowledge of binds (or joint locks)
6. Knowledge of striking in the most dangerous places
7. Knowledge of throwing your opponent
8. Knowledge of dislocating arms and legs.

I think this is quite straightforward: a good wrestler needs strength and speed, and the specific skills of ways of gripping, breaking limbs, locks, strikes, and throws. The dislocations are in practice not easy to distinguish from the breaks – the most common way to break an arm in unarmed combat is to dislocate the elbow with a hyperextension. So this feels like Fiore wanted eight things for memorisation purposes, and perhaps to go nicely with the four guards, and added in dislocations to make up the numbers.

In the Pisani Dossi MS, Fiore has seven things. He wrote:

> *Lo abraçar vole* ☒ *cosse zoe forteça presteça de pie, e de braçi, e prese avantaçade, e roture, e ligadure, e percusion, e lesion.*
>
> Wrestling wants seven things, thus: strength; speed of foot, and of arms; and advantageous grips; and breaks; and binds [locks]; and strikes; and wounds.

This is interesting because it's quite different to the "eight things" in the Getty ms. Strength is the same, speed is specified as being specifically of the feet and arms. Grips (prese) are the same, as are breaks and locks. But the strikes are much less specific, and *lesion*, "wounds", is quite different. What exactly does he mean by "wounds"? It would seem from the plays that for example an eye gouge might be considered more of a wound than a grip or a bind.

"Speed" and "Strength" are two of the four virtues shown in the iconic *segno* page:

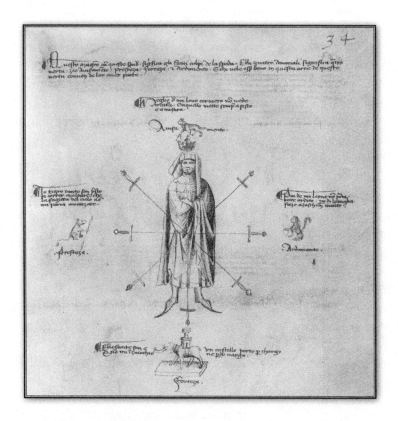

The text begins with these words:

> *Questo magistro cum queste spade significa gli Setti colpi de la spada. Elli quatro animali significa quatro vertu, zoe avisamento, presteza, forteza, e ardimento. Echi vole essere bono in questa arte de queste vertu conven de lor aver parte.*

> This master with these swords represents the seven blows of the sword. And the four animals represent four virtues, thus, foresight, speed, strength, and boldness. And whoever wishes to be good at this art must have each of them.

This is quite straightforward – here are the seven blows and here are four animals representing the four virtues anyone who trains in this art ought to cultivate: foresight, speed, strength, and boldness.

The animal above the master's head is a lynx (*lovo cerviero*), and the text reads:

> *Meglio de mi lovo cervero non vede creatura. E aquello mette sempre a sesto e a misura.*
> *Avisamento*

> No creature sees better than I, the lynx. And this [virtue] puts all in it's right place and measure.
> Foresight

The lynx is holding a pair of dividers, which represents geometry, navigation, proportion, and most of all, measurement. Accurate judgement of measure leads to better foresight.

Under the lion, the text reads:

> *Piu de mi leone non porta core ardito, pero di bataglio fazo a zaschun invito.*
> *Ardimento*

> Nobody has a bolder heart than I, the lion, I invite everyone to battle.
> Boldness

Under the elephant, the text reads:

> *Ellefante son e un castello porto per chargo*
> *E non mi inzinochio ne perdo vargo.*
> *Forteza*

> I am an elephant, and I carry a castle as my burden,
> And I do not kneel down, nor lose my stride.
> Strength

This is interesting because it suggests that strength derives from posture. You can imagine the elephant balancing the howdah on its back, and avoiding going to the ground.

Under the tiger, the text reads:

> *Io tigro tanto son presto a correr e voltare che la sagitta del cielo*
> *non mi poria avanzare.*
> *Presteza*

> I the tiger am so quick to run and turn that lightning cannot
> overtake me.
> Speed.

The advantages to a wrestler of speed and strength are obvious. So why no foresight, or boldness? It could be that wrestling occurs at such close range that you have already evinced boldness to get there, and that there is no time to predict your opponent's actions. But neither of these are convincing explanations to me, because when actually wrestling you do need to be both bold and careful.

Striking in the Most Dangerous Places

Regarding the "most dangerous places" Fiore says:

And if your enemy is unarmoured, pay attention to strike in the places more painful and more dangerous, thus in the eyes, in the nose, in the temples, under the chin, and in the flanks. And nothing less watch that you can come to the grips from the binds, whether armoured or unarmoured, that you can do one and the other.

So, the "more dangerous places" are:

1. The eyes
2. In the nose (in practice, to the septum)
3. In the temples
4. Under the chin
5. In the flanks (in practice, the floating ribs).

How to Practise

Recall that in the introduction Fiore wrote:

"Beginning the book according to the instruction of my lord Marquis, and making it so that nothing in the art is left out, that I will make sure that my lord will be please with me, through his great nobility and courtesy. And we begin with wrestling, the which is of two kinds, thus, of leisure, and of anger, thus, for your life with every trick and deception and cruelty that you can do. And of that which is done for your life, I wish to speak and show with reason, and especially to gain the grips as are used when in a fight for your life."

Fiore is explicit that there are two kinds of wrestling. That done for pleasure, and that done in anger, for your life. And he's clear that the actions he will show are to be done "with every trick and deception and cruelty that you can do". But you clearly can't train that way – you'd run out of training partners very quickly!

In the Pisani-Dossi, he wrote:

Che zoghi che se piglia de concordia le prese se fa damore e non da ira, E sopra l'arte de la brazar che se fa a guadagnar Le prese tal volta se fa da ira, e alguna volta per la vita, e sono prese e zoghi che non se po zugar de cortesia, anche sono zoghi pericolusi da zugar.

That in plays that are taken in agreement, the grips are made with love and not with anger. And about the art of wrestling that is made to gain the grips, sometimes it is done with anger and sometimes for your life, and they are grips and plays that you cannot play with courtesy, and these are also dangerous plays to practice.

E sopra quello tractaremo li zoghi avantazadi e piu forti e quilli che piu besognano in arme che senza per piu deffesa de lo homo e piu segurtade e faremo si che lezeramente se porano intendere per le parole scripte e per le figure dipente. E principiamo prima de abraçar a pe a guadagnar le prese e anchora prese facte de concordia.

And above those we will treat of the advantageous plays, and the stronger [plays], and of those that are more needed in armour than without, for more defence of man and more security, and we will do it such that one can easily understand, by the written words and by the drawn figures. And we begin first with wrestling on foot to gain the grips, and also grips made with agreement.

So, we begin with plays on foot, done "with love" not "with anger". And recall his further instruction from the Introduction (p62) that you should notice whether your opponent is stronger, bigger, older, younger, and pay attention to whether they "place themselves in the guards of wrestling", in other words, notice whether they are likely to wrestle in a familiar manner. What kind of training does it look like they've had?

FOOTWORK AND
MECHANICS

When describing Fiore's *abrazare* techniques, I'll be using a variety of technical terms that you'll need to know. These include footwork terminology from Fiore himself, as well as modern terms such as "hyperextension" and "triangle point".

Alone among the medieval sources, Fiore gives us a clear description of footwork, which he organises into three turns and four steps.

Here's what he says. I'm quoting from *From Medieval Manuscript to Modern Practice: the Longsword Techniques of Fiore dei Liberi*, p117 onwards:

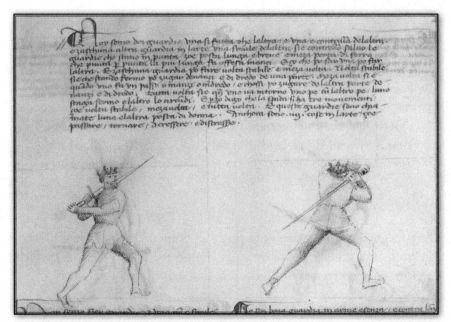

Noy semo doi guardie, una si fatta che l'altra, e una e contraria de l'altra. E zaschuna altra guardia in l'arte una simile de l'altra sie contrario, salvo le guardie che stano in punta, zoe, posta lunga e breve e meza porta di ferro che punta per punta la piu lunga fa offesa inanci. E zoe che po far una po far l'altra. E zaschuna guardia po fare volta stabile e meza volta. Volta stabile sie che stando fermo po zugar denanci e di dredo de una parte. Meza volta si e quando uno fa un passo o inanzi o indredo, e chossi po zugare de l'altra parte de inanzi e di dredo. Tutta volta sie quando uno va intorno uno pe cum l'altro pe, l'uno staga fermo e l'altro lo circundi. E perzo digo che la spada si ha tre movimenti, zoe volta stabile, meza volta, e tutta volta. E queste guardie sono chiamate l'una e l'altra posta di donna. Anchora sono iv cose in l'arte, zoe passare, tornare, acressere, e discressere.

We are two guards, one made like the other, and one is counter to the other. And [with] every other guard in the art one like the other is the counter, except for the guards that stand with the point [in the centre], thus, long guard and short, and middle iron door, that thrust against thrust the longer will strike first. And thus what one can do the other can do. And every guard can do the stable turn and the half turn. The stable turn is when, standing still, you can play in front and behind on one side. The half turn is when one makes a pass forwards or backwards, and thus can play on the other side, in front and behind. The whole turn is when one goes around one foot with the other foot, the one staying still and the other going around. And so I say that the sword also has three movements, thus stable turn, half turn, and full turn. And these guards are called, one and the other, the woman's guard. Also there are four things in the art, thus: pass, return, advance, and retreat.

Let's unpack this.

The two guards shown are both posta di donna. One is shown forward weighted, the other back weighted. I interpret the difference between them to be a volta stabile (more on that later).

1. Any two guards that are alike can counter each other.
2. Except for guards that have the point in the centre line (longa, breve, and mezana porta di ferro; more on those in the next section). This is because the longer sword will strike first. Here I'm translating punta as point (stano in punta, stand with the point), and thrust (punta per punta, thrust against thrust). The meaning is obvious whichever way you translate it though: don't stand with your point in line against someone else who has their point in line unless you have the longer sword.
3. Any similar guards can do what the guards they are like can do.
4. Every guard can do the volta stabile and the meza volta. (I use the Italian terms for technical actions, guards, etc. where possible. Refer to the glossary if you need it.)
5. The *volta stabile*: I interpret *stando fermo*, standing still, to mean without stepping, or moving a foot. As I do the volta stabile, the balls of my feet stay on the same spot on the ground. It makes no sense for a turning action to involve no movement at all, so standing still cannot mean literally 'not moving'. The *meza volta*: this is a passing action, forwards or backwards. I interpret that to include a turn of the hips and body, so you go from one side to the other.
6. The *tutta volta*: here again we have a 'fixed' foot, that, unless your legs are made of swivel-joints (top tip: they're not), must at least turn around itself for the action to occur. This supports my reading of *stando fermo* above. Simply, this is whenever you pivot on one foot by turning the other one around it. There is a video of me doing these three movements linked to further on in this chapter.
7. The sword also has three movements: stable turn, half turn, and full turn. Unfortunately there is no further discussion of this, and these terms simply aren't used in the rest of the book. Fiore will tell us to 'turn the sword', for instance in the play of the punta falsa, on f27v, but never with the qualifiers stable half or full. So I simply do not use these terms to apply to sword actions. Other instructors and interpreters do, but you should be aware that there is no evidence supporting any one interpretation of

these turns over another.

8. In case you missed it the first time: both these guards are posta di donna. Both of them. Got that?

9. There are four things in the art: pass, return, advance and retreat. (See the video mentioned shortly.)

Let me further unpack those four things:

Passare and Tornare

Passare is to pass; an unexceptional and totally uncontroversial word meaning to step with one foot going past the other. As we see from the meza volta definition, it can be done forwards and backwards.

Tornare is also a pass, but backwards. It literally means to return (please note: it in no way implies a turning action). It is not often used in the treatise, though you can find it used on f19r, in the play of the dagger defending against a sword thrust where Fiore wrote "*Lo pe dritto cum rebatter in dredo lu faro tornare.*" (see page 45 of *The Longsword Techniques of Fiore dei Liberi*). You'll notice from the video of the play that the tornare in this case isn't a full pass back: the feet come together. But I do end up with the other foot forwards, so they must pass each other.

You can also find tornare used in the text regarding posta frontale, on f24v, the pollax guard finestra, on f36r, and in the spear guard dente di zenghiaro, on f40r. Note I've not done an exhaustive search for it, as it is an uncontroversial word.

Accressere and Discressere

We know from the internal evidence that accressere (literally 'increase', which I translate as 'advance') is a movement of the front foot forwards and/or to the side, without passing, such as in the plays of the sword in one hand. Discressere (literally 'decrease') is used much more rarely. The only instance in the Getty MS is in the 7th play of the Zogho largo, in which when the player cuts for the scholar's leg, the scholar slips their foot back. I discuss this on p239 of The Longsword Techniques of Fiore dei Liberi.

Video: three turns, four steps: https://guywindsor.net/abrazare021

In conclusion then, we have three turns (stable, half, and full), and four steps (pass forwards, pass back, step forwards, step back), making seven things.

COMMON WRESTLING TERMS

Before we go on to look at Fiore's terms prese, lidagure, and roture, let me define some common wrestling terms that I'll need for describing Fiore's actions. These are:

- Crank
- Hyperextension
- Locks and Breaks
- Triangle point
- Throws

The Crank
When your opponent's arm is bent or bending, you can apply pressure to the wrist and elbow, and use their forearm as a crank handle to twist the shoulder joint. This may be done in either direction, forcing the opponent backwards or forwards.

Hyperextension
When your opponent's arm is straight or straightening, you can apply pressure to the wrist and elbow to over-straighten the arm. This puts pressure on the elbow joint, and can be used to break the arm or force the opponent to the ground. This kind of lock or break is often called an arm bar.

Lock and Break
Both cranks and hyperextensions can be used to immobilise the opponent, or to break or dislocate the joints (most commonly the elbow or the shoulder). Fiore refers in several places (f2r, f6r, f9v, f27v) to "roture e ligadure", breaks and binds. I think the distinction is primarily in the intention of the players, rather than the action itself, because any of the cranks and hyperextensions we see can be used to destroy a joint, or to hold the person still while you either wait for them to submit, or you hit them. If you are locking someone down on the ground, we would call that a pin.

Triangle Point

Human beings are bipods, which are naturally unstable. This is great for moving quickly, and much less good for standing firm. If you imagine an opponent standing normally, or in any guard, their feet will form two points of two imaginary triangles. One triangle is in front, the other behind.

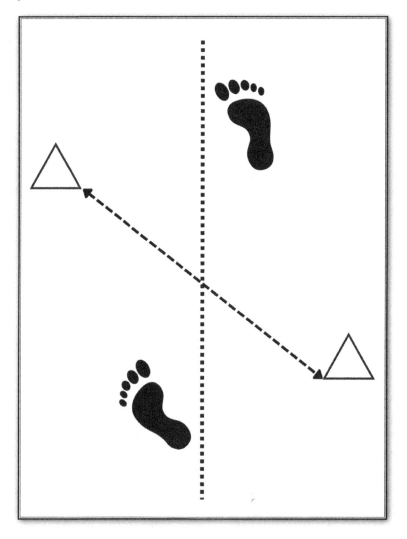

The exact form of the triangle will be affected by your opponent's hip position, and other factors, but in general the best direction to apply force when doing a wrestling technique is towards the front or rear triangle point.

In other words, in the direction where your opponent doesn't have a leg.

Throws

A throw is when you put your opponent on the ground suddenly. This is usually done by either twisting them off their feet (which Fiore shows in the third play of the abrazare), or by lifting them off their feet (which we see in the seventh). These are often accompanied by a leg lift, where you literally pick up one of your opponents feet. We see that not only in the third play, but also on horseback, where you grab their stirrup and yank it upwards.

The term 'takedown' encompasses all throws, but also leg sweeps and trips, which we wouldn't normally describe as a throw.

GRIPS, BINDS, AND BREAKS

We should also look at Fiore's uses of the terms *presa* (grip, plural: prese), *ligadura* (bind, plural ligadure), and *roture* (breaks).

Fiore uses presa (plural prese) to indicate a particular way of grabbing the opponent, and also to mean a grapple or play. The closest English term would be 'grapple', which indicates both a grabbing action (like a grappling hook for scaling castle walls like a ninja), and implies grappling, which is almost synonymous with wrestling.

The ligadure are more specific, and are usually distinguished as soprana, mezana, or sottana, which just means high, middle, and low. This literally indicates the height of your hands when you're doing the action. A high bind is done at shoulder height or above. A low bind ends up around your hip or waist height. A middle bind is done somewhere in between.

In practice, there is only one kind of ligadura mezana, which is best illustrated in the third play of the first master of dagger, here:

There are cranks and hyperextensions used in both high and low binds. Here are some examples:

Ligadura soprana crank:

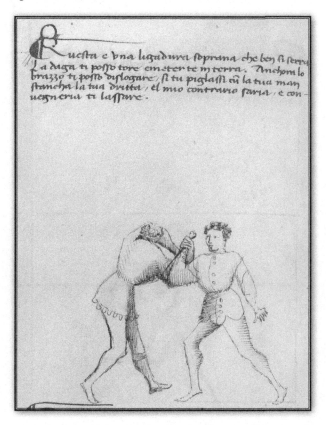

Ligadura soprana hyperextension:

Ligadura sottana crank:

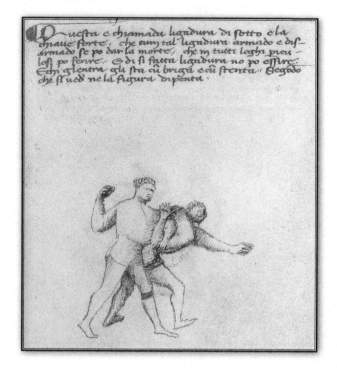

Ligadura sottana hyperextension:

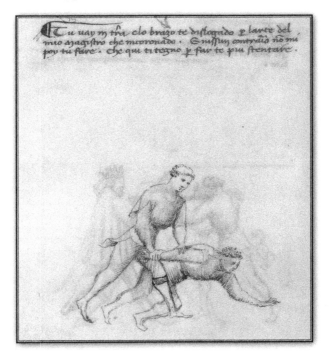

I should point out that modern martial arts are normally less specific about the height at which you do an action, and much more specific about the mechanics.

THE FOUR GUARDS OF
ABRAZARE

All of these guard images are gilded, much more so than just the crowns that we would expect. There are decorations on their doublets and belts, as well as the pommel of posta longa's dagger. Dente di zenghiaro has a gold collar, and also some kind of emblem on his chest. Porta di ferro has gold bands on his sleeves, and is wearing an ankle-length robe. The level of detail in the clothing begs the question: why are they not wearing shoes? They appear to be wrestling in their hose (which would wear out the soles of the hose very quickly).

POSTA LONGA

Io son posta longa e achosi te aspetto. E in la presa che tu mi voray fare, Lo mio brazo dritto che sta in erto, Sotto lo tuo stancho lo mettero per certo. E intrero in lo primo zogho de abrazare. E cum tal presa in terra ti faro andare. E si aquella presa mi venisse a manchare. In le altre prese che seguen vigniro intrare.

I am the long guard and I wait like this. And in the grip that you want to do to me, my right arm that is up, I will place under your left [arm] for certain. And I will enter into the first play of wrestling. And with that grip I will make you go to the ground. And if that grip fails me, I will enter the other grips that follow.

POSTA DI DENTE DI ZENGHIARO

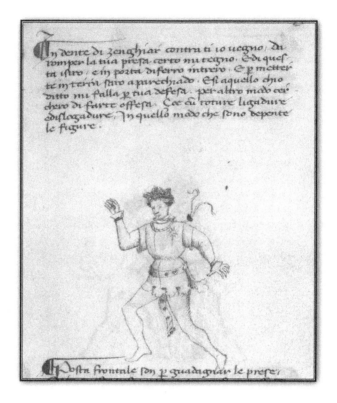

In dente di zenchiar contra ti io vegno. Da romper la tua presa certo mi tegno. E di questa isiro e in porta di ferro intrero. E per metterte in terra faro aparechiado. E si aquello chio ditto mi falla per tua defesa, per altro modo cerchero di farte offesa. Zoe cum roture, ligadure, e dislogadure, In quello modo che sono depente le figure.

I come against you in the boar's tooth. I am certain to break your grip. And I will come out of this [guard] and enter into the iron door. And I will be ready to put you on the ground. And if what I have said fails me because of your defence, I will look to make offence to you in another way. Thus, with breaks, binds, and dislocations. In the way that is shown in the figures.

It's interesting to note that the quality of the ink changes between the first and second blocks of text. I imagine the scribe changed from one batch of oak-gall ink to the next, which was more concentrated. But when we turn the page, we are back to the weaker ink. It's pure speculation, but perhaps the scribe had a supervisor who insisted he dilute the ink a bit more, to save money! (We've all had employers like that).

POSTA DI PORTA DI FERRO

In porta di ferro io ti aspetto senza mossa per guadagnar le prese a tutta mia possa. Lo zogho de Abrazare aquella e mia arte. E di lanza, Azza, Spada, e daga o grande parte. Porta di ferro son di malicie piena, chi contra me fa sempre gli do briga e pena. E a ti che contra mi voy le prese guadagnare, cum le forte prese io ti faro in terra andare.

In the iron door I wait for you without movement, to gain the grips with all my power. The play of abrazare here is my art. And I take a great part in [the plays of] the lance, axe, sword and dagger. I am the iron door full of malice, and I always give great misery and pain to those who come against me. And to you who goes against me to gain the grips, with the strong grips I will make you go to the ground.

What are the defining features of porta di ferro? Both hands are down, and the weight seems to be sinking onto the front foot. This guard is explicitly used with the weapons, and indeed we see a version of it in the spear, sword, and axe sections, as well as five variations on it in the beginning of the dagger section.

POSTA FRONTALE

Posta frontale son per guadagnar le prese. Si in questa posta vegno, tu me faray offese. Ma io mi movero di questa guardia. E cum inzegno ti movero di porta di ferro. Pezo ti faro stare che staresti in inferno. De ligadure e rotture ti faro bon merchato. E tosto si vedera chi avera guadagnato. E le prese guadagnero se non faro smemorato.

I am the frontal guard for gaining the grips. In in this guard I come, you will try to attack me. But I will move from this guard. And with cunning will move you from the iron door. Worse off you will be than if you were in hell. I will make you a good deal on locks and breaks. And quickly you will see who has gained [by the deal]. And the grips I will gain, if I am not forgetful.

These four guard positions are the foundations of the art. Literally – they are the four cornerstones of the building. Every one of the weapons guards (12 of the sword in two hands; five variations of porta di ferro for the dagger, the six guards of the sword in armour, and of the pollax, and of the spear) are all variations on these foundational four. The arms are together (porta di ferro, posta frontale) or separated (posta longa, dente di zenghiaro), extended (longa, porta di ferro, and frontale) or bent (dente di zenghiaro). And we can create any movement required by simply moving between them. Imagine you are walking down the street and see someone you wish to murder. Your hands are currently down, because you are just walking (porta di ferro). You draw your dagger and raise it to strike (dente di zenghiaro). You strike (posta longa). Or someone is attacking you with a dagger, so you extend both arms to grab theirs (frontale), and break their elbow with a *ligadura sottana* (which I'll detail later in the book, porta di ferro). The guards are positions to wait in, and the beginning, middle, and end points of all movements.

You can see the four guards, and the movements that create them, in this video:

guywindsor.net/abrazare001

THE FIRST SIX PLAYS OF ABRAZARE

I think of these first six plays as a miniature version of the entire system, covering all the major components of abrazare. Let's begin with the master and his first action.

THE FIRST TWO PLAYS: THE
MASTER AND THE ARMBAR OR
HYPEREXTENSION

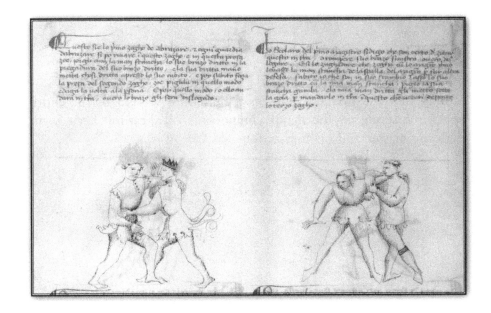

First play: the Remedy Master

Questo sie lo primo zogho de abrazare, e ogni guardia d'abrazare
si po rivare in questo zogho, e in questa presa, zoe, pigli cum la
man stancha lo suo brazo dritto in la piegadura del suo brazo
dritto, e la sua dritta mano metta chosi dritta apresso lo suo
cubito, e poy subito faza la presa del segondo zogho, zoe pigililu in
quello modo e daga la volta ala persona. E per quello modo, o ello
andara in terra, overo lo brazo gli sera dislogado.

This is the first play of wrestling, and all guards of wrestling can
arrive in this play, and in this grip, thus, grab with your left hand
his right arm in the bend of his right arm, and place your right
hand thus past his elbow, and then immediately make the grip of
the second play, thus grabbing him in that way and make a turn to
the body. And in that way, either he will go to the ground, or the
arm will be dislocated.

Second play: the hyperextension of the arm

Lo Scolaro del primo magistro si digo che son certo de zitar questo in terra, o rompere suo brazo sinistro, overo dislogare. E si lo zughadore che zogha cum lo magistro primo levasse la man stancha de la spalla del magistro per far altra defesa, subito io che son in suo scambio lasso lo suo brazo dritto cum la mia man stancha, piglo la sua stancha gamba, ela mia man dritta gli metto sotto la gola per mandarlo in terra in questo che vedeti depento lo terzo zogho.

The scholar of the first master, I say that I am certain to throw this [opponent] to the ground, or break his left arm, or dislocate [it]. And if the player that plays with the first master lifts his left hand from the master's shoulder to make some other defence, immediately I that am here in his place leave his right arm with my left hand, grab his left leg, and my right hand I place under the throat to send him to the ground in the way that you see illustrated in the third play.

The master remedies the player's attempt to grab him by controlling both of the player's elbows. Notice that the extended arm goes against a bent arm, and vice versa. This is in a sense posta longa countering dente di zenghiaro, and zenghiaro countering longa.

You break an extended arm by over-extending it, creating what's known as an arm bar, or a hyperextension. The player's hand is anchored against the master's neck, and the master's forearm applies pressure to the elbow, ideally just above the head of the radius bone.

The scholar's foot position is interesting. You can get there by either passing your right foot through in the direction of the arm bar, or you can swing your left foot around behind you in a tutta volta. For many years the former was my default interpretation, but since creating my Medieval Wrestling course with Jessica Finley, I've moved over to doing the tutta volta by preference.

You can see this on video here: guywindsor.net/abrazare002

The Third Play: the rear throw

Questo scolaro che denanzi de mi dise ben lo vero che de la sua presa convene che vegna in questa per metterlo in terra, overo dislogarglil brazo stancho. Anchora digo che si lo zugadore levasse la man stancha de la spalla del magistro che lo magistro, che lo magistro[1] rivaria al terzo zogho simile mente chomo vedeti depento. Si che per lo primo zogho e per lo segondo che uno proprio zogho, ello magistro lo manda in terra cum lo volto, e lo terzo lo manda cum se Spalle in terra.

---

1   Note that "che lo magistro" is repeated, a scribal error.

That scholar that is before me say well the truth, that from his grip I have come to this one to put him on the ground, or to dislocate his left arm. Also I say that if the player lifts his left hand from the master's shoulder, the master will arrive in the third play, as you see illustrated. So in the first play and the second, which is one of his own plays, the master sends him to the ground on his face, and in the third he sends him to the ground on his shoulder.

This is a really interesting moment in the source, because Fiore explicitly tells us to change what we're doing based on our opponent's actions. He says that if they take their hand off your shoulder, you should throw them on their back, instead of forwards onto their face. If practising this, do NOT let your partner fall, unless they are trained to fall this way.

You can see this on video here: guywindsor.net/abrazare003

THE FOURTH PLAY: OTHER FOOT FORWARDS

Questo e lo quarto zogho de abrazare che liziero se lo scolaro po metter lo zugadore in terra. E se non lo po metter per tal modo in terra, ello zerchera altri zogi e prese como si po fare per diversi modi chomo vedereti al dredo noy depento. Che posseti ben savere che gli zoghi non sono eguali ne le prese rare volte e pero chi non a bona presa se la guadagni piu presto chel po per non lassare avantazo al inimigho suo.

This is the fourth play of abrazare, [in] which the scholar can easily put the player on the ground. And if he can't put him on the ground in this way, he will look for other plays and grips that can be done in various ways as you will see illustrated below. You should know well that the plays are not the same, and the grips are rarely the same, so if one doesn't have a good grip, gain one as quickly as possible, so as to not let the advantage go to your enemy.

You can see this on video here: guywindsor.net/abrazare004

This play covers the problem of your opponent having the 'wrong' leg forward. Because of this, their line of weakness will change from your front right/back left, to front left/back right.

The wrestling story so far goes like this: control their elbows. Break their arm by turning into their line of weakness. If their elbow isn't available take their head. If their feet are the other way round, go to the other diagonal.

This is fascinating. There is one brief line about what to do in this position (throw the opponent), and the admonition that if you can't, then do something else, and quickly!

To my mind, the principle difference in this play from the ones that came before it, is the foot position of the player. In the first three plays he is left foot forwards, and now he is shown with his right foot forwards. The net effect of this is to change the line that the scholar has to work on. Previously, the line ran diagonally back to the left and forwards to the right (as we see in the actions of the second and third plays). Now the line runs forward to the left and backwards to the right.

THE FIFTH PLAY: THE BEAR HUG

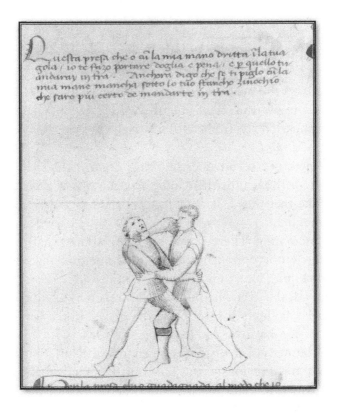

Questa presa che o cum la mia mano dritta in la tua gola, io te fazo portare doglia e pena, e per quello tu anderai in terra. Anchora digo che se ti piglo cum la mia mane mancha sotto lo tuo stancho zinochio che faro piu certo de mandarte in terra.

This grip that I have with my right hand in your throat, I make to you to bring suffering and pain, and by which you will go to the ground. Also I say that if I grip you with my left hand under your left knee I will be more certain to send you to the ground.

In plays one to three, the player has their left foot forwards, you have your right. In the fourth play, the player has switched legs. Now in the fifth, we look at the problem of the player having their left foot forwards again (so the line of weakness will be back where it was in the first three plays), but they have both hands round your waist. What should you do?

Following the example of the third and fourth plays, you know that if the elbow is unavailable, you go to the face. So, with your left hand gripping their right hip, press your right hand to their left cheek, turning their head, and twist them to your right.

You can see this on video here: guywindsor.net/abrazare005

The Sixth Play: the Counter-Remedy: push the elbow

Io son contrario del quinto zogo denanzi apresso. E si digo che se cum la mia mane dritta levo lo suo brazo et la sua mane che al volto mi fa impazo, faro gli dar volta per modo chio lo metero in terra, per modo che vedeti qui depento, overo che guadagnaro presa o ligadura, e de tuo abrazar faro pocha cura.

I am the counter to the fifth play, immediately before me. And I say that with my right hand I lift your arm and your hand that is offending my face, I make you turn in such a way that I put you on the ground, in the way that you see illustrated here, or I will gain a grip or lock, and I am not bothered by your wrestling.

This is the first counter remedy that we see in the entire treatise. When doing it in practice, the first thing that leaps out at us is that the text and illustrations don't line up. In the fifth play the scholar is shown using his right hand to go for the throat, which is also specified in the text. But here, the player is using his left hand against the counter-remedy master's face. I think the lesson is in the text: "your hand that is offending my face". Whichever one that is, that's the elbow to push.

You can see this on video here: guywindsor.net/abrazare006

Notice that this play, the counter-remedy, is basically the same idea as the second play – push the elbow. You might also notice that you are continually using your bent, dente di zenghiaro/boar's tooth arm to control their extended, posta longa/long guard arm.

The First Six Plays as a Group

The first six plays of abrazare form a mini-system that, once learned, will pay dividends as you move through the rest of the system. This is what they represent:

1. The Remedy Master. A specific response to a specific threat, in this case controlling the attacker's elbows when they grab you.
2. The First Scholar: continuing the action of the Remedy Master to its proper conclusion, breaking the extended arm by hyper-extending it.
3. The Second Scholar: if the companion removes their hand, or bends their elbow, the hyperextension won't work, so redirect your hand from their elbow to their face, and throw them.
4. The Third Scholar: if the companion has their other foot forwards, their lines of strength and weakness change, so you take them down in the other direction.
5. The Fourth Scholar: if the companion has their arms around your waist, neither arm is available for breaking, so you go straight to their face for a takedown.
6. The Counter-Remedy Master: whichever hand is coming for your face, push the elbow up to turn the companion.

We can summarise this as a set of principles: control the opponent's weapon(s). Go for the available target. If the available target changes, change your approach. Act in their line of weakness, which is largely determined by their foot positions. Counter by controlling whichever of their weapons offers the most immediate threat.

SETTING UP AND
FINISHING THE PLAYS

Now that we have seen the first six plays, we should pause to think about how they should be set up, and finished.

In the plays of the sword (and other weapons), it's quite clear how the situation for the plays can arise – you have either been attacked with a cut or a thrust, or you have attacked your opponent similarly. But what about the wrestling?

Fiore doesn't discuss how we get into the situation shown in the first master. What preceded this position? Nobody just walks up to you and arranges themselves so that you can put your hands on their elbows.

There are several possible beginnings. In a pre-arranged wrestling match, there is often a standard starting position. In the case of collar-and-elbow wrestling, the name of the wrestling style *is* the starting position. You have one hand on their collar, and one on their elbow, and your opponent has the same. Modern Greco-Roman wrestling begins with one wrestler on their hands and knees, and the other, holding them around the waist. It seems unlikely, given the *a l'oltranza* nature of Fiore's wrestling that the start point is intended to be co-operative. We could get there from a mutual elbow hold (a very common start to a wrestling match), from which the player is going for the head. We could also get there from the player grabbing the master's collar to punch (or stab!) them in the stomach. And it is also possible that the master's position is intended to convey the more general message to control the opponents elbows.

FINISHING THE PLAYS

Fiore shows the plays up to the point right before your partner gets injured. We never see (as we do in other sources) swords going through bodies, blood spurting, body parts lopped off, maimed opponents lying on the ground, and so on. So it seems likely that he is deliberately showing the point in the play right before injury occurs. It is perfectly correct then to take the play to that point and then stop. But it is also good and common practice to modify the play to allow a more complete execution of it. For instance, you can convert an action that would break the arm into a friendly throw.

PLAYS 7-16 OF ABRAZARE

THE SEVENTH PLAY: A CROSSED LEG GRAB

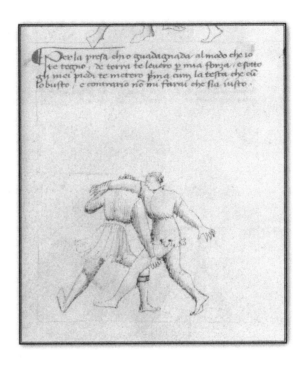

Per la presa chio guadagnada al modo che io te tegno, de terra te levero per mia forza, e sotto gli miei piedi te metero prima cum la testa che cum lo busto, e contrario non mi farai che sia iusto.

By the grip that I have gained in the way that I have you, I will lift you off the ground by my strength, and place you under my feet, first with the head, then the body, and you will not be able to counter me, in a way that would fit.

In practice, this works best if your partner is pushing their right hand towards you. You can then simply redirect it up a bit, and step underneath quite easily.

You can see this on video here: guywindsor.net/abrazare007

The Eighth Play: thumb under the ear

Lo dedo poles te tegno sotta la tua orechia che tanta doglia senti per quello che tu andarai in terra senza dubito, overo altra presa ti faro o ligadura che sara piu fiera che tortura. Lo contrario che fa lo sesto zogho contra lo quinto quello che gli metti la mano sotto lo chubito, aquello si po far a me tal contrario senza nessuno dubito.

The thumb I have under your ear, you will feel so much pain from it that you will go to the ground without doubt, or I will do another grip or bind that will be worse than torture. The counter that the sixth play makes against the fifth, the one that places the hand under the elbow, that counter you could do to me without any doubt.

If you wiggle your thumb under your ear behind your jawbone you will find a sensitive spot. That's the target that I think Fiore has in mind. Done hard and fast this is very nasty, but not actually dangerous, unlike other options such as going for the eyes.

You can see this on video here: guywindsor.net/abrazare008

THE NINTH PLAY: ESCAPE FROM A HOLD FROM THE REAR

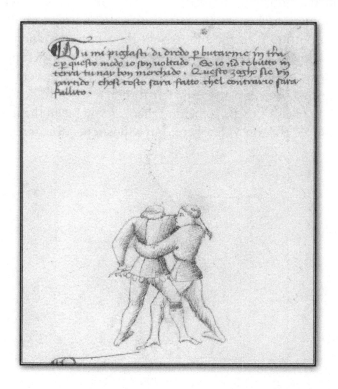

Tu mi piglasti di dredo per butarme in terra e per questo modo io son voltado. Se io non te butto in terra tu nay bon mechado. Questo zogho sie un partido, chosi tosto sara fatto chel contrario sara fallito.

You grabbed me from behind to throw me to the ground, and in this way I have turned. If I do not throw you to the ground you will get a good deal. This play is a technique that is so fast that is it done such that the counter will fail.

This technique must be done quickly, or (the implication is) that the initial attacker will counter it. Note the use of the term *partido* (technique) alongside *zogho* (play). This play is a technique that... This usage highlights the liberties I am taking with the title of this book: I should really call all of these actions "plays", because that's what Fiore does, and the implications of the term are different to "techniques". But newcomers to historical martial arts don't understand the term "play", so putting it in the title would be counter-productive.

This is a lovely examination of basic mechanics. By getting your leg behind theirs, their grip on you becomes a throw on them. The trick to it is shifting your hips to your left to make space to get your right foot from in front of them, to behind them as you see in the illustration.

You can see this on video here: guywindsor.net/abrazare009

The Tenth Play: The Gambarola

Questo sie un zogho da Gambarola che non e ben sigura chosa nel abrazare. E se alguno pur vol fare la gambarola, faza la cum forza e presta mente.

This is a tripping play that is not a safe thing of wrestling. And if anyone wants to do the tripping play, do it with strength and quickly.

Gambarola has come to be used as a technical term for this play – we call it "the gambarola". But it literally means 'tripping'. Fiore states that it is not a safe technique, presumably because either player could do it: neither has a clear advantage. And so to make it work you need to do it quickly and strongly.

You can see this on video here: guywindsor.net/abrazare010

The Eleventh Play: the full Nelson

Questo sie un partido e sie una strania presa a tegner uno a tal modo che non se po defendere. Lo contrario sie che quello che tegnudo vada al piu tosto chel po apressol muro o altro ligname e volti se per modo chello faza a choluy chelo tene romper la testa ela schena in lo ditto muro overo ligname.

This is a technique and it is a strange grip to hold someone in such a way that they cannot defend themselves. The counter is that the one who is held goes as quickly as they can against a wall or other construction [lit. 'wooden thing'] and turns so that he breaks the head and the back of the one who is holding him against the said wall or construction.

This technique is a mainstay of modern wrestling, and is known as the full nelson. Getting into it can be tricky. I get there by pushing the player's left elbow up with my right hand, and hooking under their left arm with my left. I grab the back of their neck with my left hand and yank it down and to the left. A bit of a smack to the right flank with my right hand gives me a moment of distraction letting me get my right arm hooked up under their right, and the hold is complete.

I was taught a counter to this many years ago where you break one of the opponent's little fingers, and use that to lever your way out. Smacking their back against a wall works best if there is something sharp sticking out of it. Otherwise they may be able to hold on.

You can see this on video here: guywindsor.net/abrazare011

THE TWELFTH PLAY: KNEE TO THE GROIN

Questo fere lo compagno cum lo zinochio in gli chogloni per avere piu avantazo di sbaterlo in terra. Lo contrario sie che subito che lo compagno tra cum lo zinochio per ferirlo in gli cogloni, chello debia cum la man dritta piglare la ditta gamba sotto lo zinochio e sbaterlo in terra.

This strike that the companion makes with the knee in the nuts to have more advantage in throwing him on the ground. The counter is that immediately that the companion comes with the knee to strike him in the nuts, he must with the right hand grab the said leg under the knee and throw him to the ground.

Interestingly, this knee strike is done with the front, weighted, leg, which is much more difficult, and doesn't strike so hard, but is much faster. This makes it much harder to feel coming, and thus counter. It's a distraction, not a finishing move, to set you up for the throw.

You can see this on video here: guywindsor.net/abrazare012

THE THIRTEENTH PLAY: NOSE SMASH

Per zo che tu me ha piglado cum li toi brazi de sotto gli miei, trambe le mie man te fierino in lo volto. E si tu fossi ben armado cum questo zogho io faria lassado. Lo contrario di questo zogho sie che si lo scolaro che ven inzuriado del zugadore in lo volto, metta se la sua man dritta sotto lo cubito del zugadore zoe del brazo sinistro e penza lu forte, e lu scolar rimara in sua liberta.

Because you have grabbed me with your arms under mine, [with] both of my hands I will strike you in the face. And if you had been armoured, with this play I would be released. The counter of this play is that if the scholar that became injured by the player in the face, places his right hand under the elbow of the player, thus of the left arm, and pushes it hard, the scholar would remain free.

There are some interesting things being done with the language here. Fiore is going to great lengths to specify who is doing what to whom, but leaving out any detail about the execution of the technique. Compare this with the text from the same play from the Pisani Dossi:

In tuo naso fazo tanta pena e doia
Che a lassarme tosto pera tua voia

In your nose I make so much pain and suffering,
That you will want to let go of me quickly.

It doesn't specify the set-up with the arms at all, but it does specify the target: the nose. Recalling 'striking in the places most dangerous' from the introduction, we've already seen the nerve cluster under the ear, and the groin, and now we have the nose.

In practice, it's best to strike diagonally upwards under the nose, at the angle shown by the scholar's arms. I double up my hands such that the webs of both thumbs line up with each other, and use the web to shove up against the septum.

You can see this on video here: guywindsor.net/abrazare013

THE FOURTEENTH PLAY:
COUNTER TO THE NOSE SMASH

Lo contrario del xiii io fazo. Le soy mani del mio volto sono partide. E per lo modo chio lo preso e si lo tegno. Si ello non va in terra prendere grande disdegno.

I make the counter to the 13 [th play]. Your hands from my face are separated. And by the way that I have the grip, and so I have him. If he does not go to the ground, I will be greatly disgraced.

The first thing we note is that the counter is illustrated as pushing the player's right elbow, not the left specified in the text to the 13th play. So which is correct?

The Pisani-Dossi shows pushing the left forearm:

And it also has the leg lift that isn't mentioned in the text for this play, or the 13th. It would make more sense to me that you would at least start with your hand on their left elbow, but you might need to switch it to get the leg lift. I usually get here by pushing up with the closest hand (eg my right hand on their left elbow) then add my other hand (eg my left hand to the same left elbow), freeing up my right hand for the leg lift. The turn that you give to their body with the elbow push unweights the leg, making it easy to lift.

You can see this on video here: guywindsor.net/abrazare014

THE FIFTEENTH PLAY: HANDS TO FACE

> *Se tu pigli uno cum trambe li toy brazi de sotto va cum le toy*
> *mane al suo volto segondo vedi che io fazo, e mazormente sello e*
> *discoverto lo volto. Anchora puo tu vegnire in lo terzo zogho de*
> *Abrazare.*

> If you grab someone with both of your arms from below [i.e.
> under their arms] go with both your hands to their face, as you see
> that I do, and especially if he has uncovered his face. Also you can
> come into the third play of wrestling.

What is the target? As the counter, in the next play, is to stick your
thumb in the opponent's eye, I think the target here is a strike below

the chin. The lesson of this play is I think mechanical. If your hands are low, and they go high, if you also go high you will dislodge their hands by pushing their forearms upwards with yours. You don't need to think about it: if you just send your hands to their face, your arms will dislodge theirs automatically.

You can see this on video here: guywindsor.net/abrazare015

THE SIXTEENTH PLAY: THE EYE GOUGE

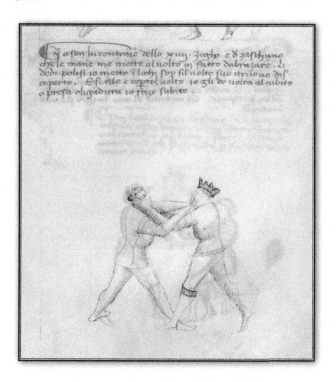

Io son lu contrario dello xiv zogho, e d' zaschuno che le mane me mette al volto in fatto d'abrazare. Li dedi polisi io metto in lochi soy sil volto suo itruovo discoperto. E si ello e coperto l volto io gli do volta al cubito o presa oligadura io fazo subito.

I am the counter to the fourteenth play, and to any [play] in which the hands are placed on my face in a wrestling action. The thumbs I place in the eyes, if I find his face uncovered. And if he has covered his face I give a turn to his elbow, or I do a grip or bind immediately.

Covered/uncovered probably refers to armour, as well as to the possibility that the player is protecting their face with their arms in some way. This is very clearly not a "grip of love!". This book is not a training manual, but just in case you are walking through the plays with a friend, do not under any circumstances practice this play without eye protection. It only takes one small slip, or a nick with a fingernail, to do horrific, permanent, damage.

You can see this on video here: guywindsor.net/abrazare016

PLAYS 17-20: THE BASTONCELLO

WHAT IS A BASTONCELLO?

A bastoncello, literally "small stick", has been carried by authority figures since antiquity. It usually symbolises some kind of martial or policing authority. For instance we see (Holy Roman) Emperor Charles V (1500-1558) choosing to be portrayed with one here:

It is no coincidence that there is a statue of Fiore's patron Niccolo d'Este, Marquis of Ferrara (1383-1441), which shows him holding a bastoncello while mounted. The statue was originally erected in 1451, but was destroyed by Napoleon's troops in 1796. This reproduction was erected in 1926:

Its modern incarnation is the Field Marshal's baton, still presented to Field Marshals of the British Army today (most recently in 2014). This etching shows the various batons presented to the Duke of Wellington (1769-1852) over his career:

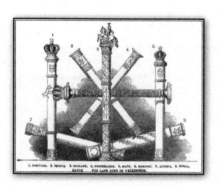

So it is not so strange that we would find Fiore showing techniques that Niccolo could (for example) defend himself with against assassination, using something he was likely to be holding.

The Seventeenth Play of Abrazare, or first of Bastoncello

Guarda che cum uno bastoncello io te tegno per lo collo ligado, E in terra ti voglio butare, pocha braga per questo ho a fare. Che se io te volesse pezo trattare in la forte ligadura te faria entrare. Ello contrario non mi porissi fare.

Watch that with a bastoncello I hold you bound at the neck, and I want to throw you on the ground. I have little difficulty in doing that. If I wanted to treat you worse I would make you enter the strong lock. You could not do the counter to me.

The mystery of this play is, what is the player doing? Why is he apparently trying to grab the scholar's leg with both hands? And why start with that against someone holding a stick?

I think the answer is that it's a general instruction: if their hands are low, go high (as we've seen so many times before). And if you have a bastoncello, trap the neck. You do it by holding it in a reverse grip with your right hand and hooking the neck, then grab the bastoncello with your left hand, ideally from underneath your right forearm. This gives you a huge amount of leverage. You can break the neck, or throw, or choke them out. (Please don't, it's both immoral and illegal.)

This is a truly awful play to be on the receiving end of.

You can see this on video here: guywindsor.net/abrazare017

The Eighteenth play of Abrazare, or second of Bastoncello

Stu fossi ben armado in questo zogo piu tosto te faria. Considerando che to preso cum uno bastonzello tra le gambe. Tu sta a cavallo e pocho ti po durare che cum la schena ti faro versare.

If you were well armoured I would do this play to you very quickly. Thinking that I have got you with a bastoncello between your legs. You are riding and you can withstand little [before] I make you go backwards onto your back.

As with the previous play, the question is what does the player think he's doing? I suppose it could be an action initiated by the scholar. In any case, you push the player back with your left hand in their throat, and hook your bastoncello between their legs. This stops them taking a step back, and so they fall. I would tend to slam my forearm into their groin when doing this, to make the follow up easier.

You can see this on video here: guywindsor.net/abrazare018

THE NINETEENTH PLAY OF ABRAZARE, THIRD OF BASTONCELLO

Del Sesto Re ch'e rimedio di daga e contra per questo modo cum sua daga di quello son Scolaro. E per suo honore fazo tal coverta cum questo bastoncello. E subito mi levo in pe, e fazo gli zoghi del mio magistro. Questo che fazo cum lo bastoncello iolfaria cum un p capuzo. El contrario d'l mio magistro sie mio contrario.

Of the sixth king that is a remedy of dagger is [the] counter in this way with the dagger, of that [king] I am a scholar. And in his honour I make the counter with this bastoncello. And immediately I get up on my feet, and make the plays of my master. This that I do with the bastoncello I could do with a hood. And the counter of my master is my counter.

The lesson of this play is that you can defend yourself against a dagger with something connecting your hands, like a stick or a hood. I've also done it with a piece of rope, a belt, and a bandanna. Interestingly, Fiore confuses two dagger masters here. The eighth master parries a low blow with the dagger held in both hands (like the bastoncello is here), and the sixth parries a high blow (as we see in the next play).

The eighth master of the dagger:

Lotavo magistro son e incroso cum mia daga. E questo zogo e bon in arme e senzarme. E li miei zogi sono posti alchuni denanzi alchuni di dredo. Lo zogo chi me denanzi zoe lo quarto zogo zoe chi fere le zugadore in la man cum la punta di sua daga per lo simile poria ferir costuy di sotta mano, como ello lo fere di sopra. Anchora poria piglar la sua mano in la zuntura cum la mia man stancha, e cum la dritta lo poria ben ferire. Segondo che trovarete dredo di mi lo nono scolaro del nono magistro, che fere lo

zugadore nel petto. Anchora poria fare lo ultimo zogo che dredo abandonando la mia daga.

I am the eighth master and I cross with my dagger. And this play is good in armour and without armour. And my plays are put some after [me], some before. The play that is before, so the fourth play, so the one that strikes the player in the hand with the point of his dagger, in the same way he could strike his under-arm [blow], as he struck from above. Also I could grab his hand in the joint, with my left hand, and with the right I could strike him well. According to what you will find below me in the ninth play of the ninth master, that strikes the player in the chest. Also I could do the last play [of the ninth master] that is below, abandoning my dagger.

Note that Fiore is saying that just as the stab to the hand can be done against an overhand blow, it can also be done against an underarm blow. Interestingly, the eighth master's scholars are the counter-remedy, and variations on the cover itself (covering with left forearm, holding your left wrist with your right hand; or covering with your forearms crossed). It is assumed you already know a whole lot of dagger techniques.

Executing this play is quite straightforward. You sit on your bench, minding your own business, and when the player comes to stab you, block it from above with the bastoncello against the blade of the dagger. My favourite continuation from there is to grab their wrist with my left hand and strip the dagger out of their hand with the bastoncello.

You can see this on video here: guywindsor.net/abrazare019

THE TWENTIETH PLAY OF ABRAZARE, OR FOURTH OF BASTONCELLO

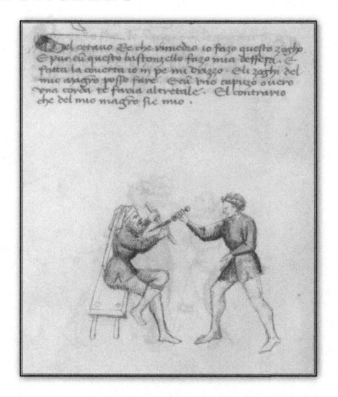

Del octavo Re che rimedio io fazo questo zogho. E pur cum questo bastonzello fazo mia deffesa. E fatta la coverta io in pe mi drizzo. Eli zoghi del mio magistro posso fare. E cum uno capuzo overo una corda te faria altretale. El contrario che del mio magistro sie mio.

Of the eighth King that is remedy I make this play. And by this bastoncello I make my defence. And having made the cover I get up on my feet. And the plays of my master I can do. And with a

hood or a rope I would make [the defence against] you just the
same. The counter of my master is [also] mine.

Recalling that Fiore has the masters switched here, we need the sixth
master of the dagger.

The sixth master of the dagger:

*Sesto Magistro che son digo che questa coverta e fina in arme e
senzarme. E cum tal coverta posso covrire in ogni parte. E intrare
in tutte ligadure. E far prese e ferire segondo che gli scolari miei
vignirano a ferire finire. E questa coverta fazza zaschuno mio
scolaro. E poy faza li zoghi dredo che si po fare.*

Sixth Master am I, I say that this cover is good in armour and out
of armour. And with this cover I can cover on all sides. And enter

in all locks. And make grips and strikes according to my scholars, they will come to [the] strike finish. And this cover is made by each of my scholars. And I can make the plays below, that can be done.

The next play, the Sixth Master's first scholar, has him grab the player's wrist, and strike with his own dagger, and the next has another strike with the scholar's dagger. Given that you are not holding a dagger, you'd be better served with the fourth play (third scholar), which is a disarm:

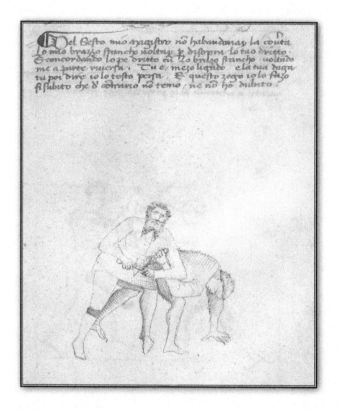

Del Sesto mio magistro non habandonay la coverta. Lo mio brazzo stancho voltar per disopra lo tuo dritto. E concordando lo pe dritto cum Lo brazo stancho, voltado me a parte riversa. Tu e mezo ligado, e la tua daga tu poi dire io lo tosto persa. E questo zogo io lo fazo si subito che d' contrario non temo, ne non ho dubito.

Of the Sixth my master, his cover, I do not abandon. My left arm I turn above your right. And co-ordinating my right foot with my left arm, I turned myself to the backhand side. You are half bound, and your dagger you will say "I lost it quickly". And this play I do so quickly that I do not fear the counter, of that I have no doubt.

This is my favourite continuation. You reach up with extended arms to parry the downwards stab, rising to your feet, and stepping to the outside (your left against a right-handed blow), rolling the bastoncello over their forearm to strip the dagger out of their hand.

You can see this on video here: guywindsor.net/abrazare020

WHAT'S MISSING FROM THE ABRAZARE PLAYS?

As we have seen, these plays exist within the context of the entire treatise, so some wrestling-type actions are only shown later on (in the dagger section, for instance). But even taking the entire treatise into account, any wrestler will look at these plays and ask at least the following questions:

1. Where is the groundwork: Why don't we see any plays done from the ground?
2. Where are the sacrifice throws?
3. Where are the over-the-shoulder throws?
4. Where are the leg sweeps?

There is no single answer, and the fact is that all of these actions do exist in (reasonably) contemporary German sources. But I should stress that they are not nearly so common as we find them in modern wrestling practice. My guess is that modern competition rule sets and environments (rings, mats etc.) explain much of the discrepancy.

Groundwork

Codex I.6.4.3, known as Codex Lew, and published in transcription and translation by Dierk Hagedorn as *Jude Lew: das Fechtbuch* has an entire section (pp 221-236) on Unterhalten ja Aufstehen (Holding Down and Getting Up), has a range of actions done on the ground, such as:

"If he falls on the back, fall with the right knee between his legs and seize his right arm in your left knee bend. Sit down on it and grab his left hand with your right hand. Push it under his neck, and hold him fast with your left. Work with the dagger with the right." (p. 225)

As you can see, this involves following your opponent to the ground, and murdering him with a dagger. It's not strictly unarmed.

There is also an entire section on Ringen, wrestling, attributed to Master Ott, pp 271-291, which contains a lot of similar actions to Fiore's abrazare, but none of our missing components.

The Bauman Fechtbuch (Cod. ⊠.6.4°.2; often called Codex Wallerstein) also has several holds done on the ground, including ways of pinning several opponents, such as here in folio 74r, in which you pin three prisoners at once! My friends who have tried this say it is appallingly painful and effective.

The text as translated by Gregorz Zabinski and Bartlomiez Walczak (*Codex Wallerstein*, 2002) reads:

Then, a very good hold because you can hold three captured men whether they already have irons on [or not], and it is very painful whether one wants to cause pain to someone, as it is depicted here. Such a necessity happens often.

Personally, I've never found it necessary to restrain three prisoners at once, but who am I to argue with the text?

Sacrifice throw
Folio 41 of the Bauman Fechtbuch shows a sacrifice throw:

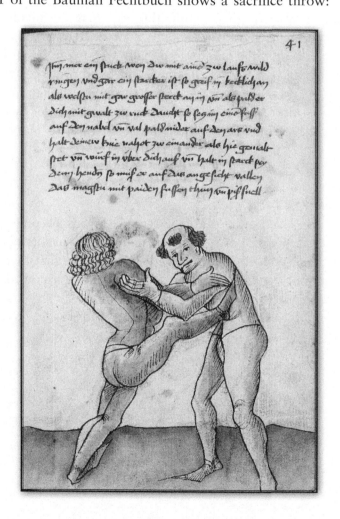

The text as translated by Gregorz Zabinski and Bartlomiez Walczak (*Codex Wallerstein*, 2002) reads:

So, one more trick: if you want to fight someone by running at him and he is quite strong: boldly grasp him any way you want with a lot of force. When he pulls you back with force, put your foot into his stomach and fall down quickly onto your seat; hold your knees close together, as depicted here; and throw him over you, holding his hands tightly so that he has to fall on his face. You can act with both feet, and you should be quick.

Over-the-shoulder throws

The problem with over-the-shoulder throws is that they involve turning into the opponent, getting within reach of their other hand. This is dangerous in a mortal situation, especially when you may not be sure whether they have a weapon in the other hand. But they have their place, and we do see them in the German sources, though the forward hip throw is more common. You can quite easily enter an over-the-shoulder throw from the cover of the first or fourth masters of the dagger.

Leg sweeps

'Sweep the leg!"

Thanks to The Karate Kid, the leg sweep has become almost a catch-phrase in martial arts, and it certainly does have its place. Fiore doesn't explicitly mention it anywhere. My guess is that there's a risk of your armour catching on theirs if you do it in armour. But again the German sources do provide examples.

ABRAZARE ON HORSEBACK

The first sixteen abrazare plays represent the entire body of completely unarmed and unarmoured combat on foot. I have researched the mounted wrestling plays, and they are very horse-specific; techniques include pulling up your opponent's stirrup to throw them, and grabbing the opponent's horse's bridle and nudging their horse's rump with your horse's chest or shoulder, to throw the entire horse-rider combination to the ground. While knowing the on-foot wrestling will certainly help your mounted wrestling, the mounted wrestling isn't going to help your wrestling on foot.

But you want to see it anyway?

OK, since you asked nicely...

I haven't created video clips of this yet, though I plan to produce a volume on the mounted plays in this series, and will shoot these plays once that happens. I haven't practised these plays, so can't comment authoritatively on how they should be done.

Questo e zogho de Abrazare zoe zogho de brazi, e si fa per tal modo. Quando uno ti fuzi dela parte stancha tu gli ven apresso. Cum la man dritta tu lo pigli in le sguanze dello bazinetto, e se ello e disarmado per gli cavigli, overo per lo brazo dritto per dredo le soy spalle. Per tal modo faralo rivisare, che in terra lo farai andare.

This is a play of wrestling, thus a play of the arms, and it is done in this way. When one runs away from you on their left side, you get close. With the right hand you grab him in the cheek piece of the bascinet, and if he is unarmoured by the hair, or by the right arm behind his shoulder. In that way you will make him go backwards, such that you will make him go to the ground.

Questo e contrario del zogho ch'e denazi ne val per tal modo,
questo contrario cum tal presa se fa zoe subito quando ello per
dredo lo piglia, La man de la briglia debia subito scambiare, e cum
lo brazo stancho per tal modo lo de pigtlare.

This is the counter to the play that is before, that is done in this
way, this counter with this grip is done, thus, immediately when
grabs him from behind, the bridle hand must be immediately
changed, and with the left arm in this way he must be grabbed.

Questo scolaro vole buttar questo da cavallo, zoe chello lo piglia per la staffa, e levalo in erto. Se ello non va in terra, in aere stara per certo, salvio s'ello non e al cavallo ligado, questo zogho non po essi fallado. E se ello non a lo pe in la staffa, per lo collo del pe lo piglia che piu vale levandolo in erto come denanzi ditto. Fate quello ch'e denanzi qui scritto.

This scholar wishes to to throw this mounted person, thus he grabs him by the stirrup, and lifts it up. If he does not go to the ground, he will be in the air for sure. Unless he is tied to the horse, this play cannot fail. And if he does not have his foot in the stirrup, grab him by the neck of the foot [ie ankle] that is better at lifting him up, as said before. Do that which is written before this.

Lo contrario del zogho denanzi qui e parechiado, che se uno ti piglia per la staffa overo per lo pe, buttagli lo brazo al collo, e questo subito far si de. E per tal modo lo poray discavalcare da cavallo. S'tu fa questo ello andera in terra senza fallo.

The counter to the play before me appears here, that if one grabs you by the stirrup or by the foot, throw your arm to his neck, and do it immediately. And in this way you could unhorse him from the horse. If you do this he will go to the ground without fail.

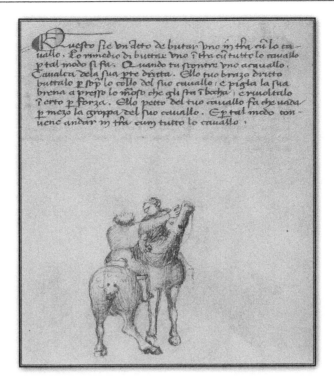

Questo sie un atto de butar uno in terra cum lo cavallo. Lo rimedio di buttar uno in terra cum tutto lo cavallo per tal modo si fa. Quando tu scontre uno a cavallo, cavalca dela sua parte dritta. Ello tuo brazo dritto buttalo per sopra lo collo del suo cavallo, e pigla la sua brena a presso lo morso che gli sta in bocha, e rivoltalo in erto per forza. Ello petto del tuo cavallo fa che vada per meza la groppa del suo cavallo. E per tal modo convene andar in terra cum tutto lo cavallo.

This is an act of throwing someone to the ground with the horse. The remedy of throwing someone to the ground with the whole horse is done in this way. When you encounter someone on horseback, ride to their right side. Your right arm throw over the neck of their horse, and grab their bridle close to the bit that is in the [horse's] mouth, and twist it up with force. Make the chest of your horse go to the middle of the crupper [rump] of his horse. And in this way you make him go to the ground with the whole horse.

Questo sie lo contrario di questo zogho qui denanzi che vole buttar in terra lo compagno cum tutto lo cavallo. Questa e lizera chosa da cognossere che quando lo scolaro butta lo brazo per sopra lo collo del cavallo per piglar la brena, de subito ello gli de buttar el brazo lo zugador al collo dello scolaro, e per forza ello conven lassar. Segondo vedeti qui depento si debia fare.

This is the counter to this play that is before, that wants to throw to the ground the companion with the whole horse. This is an easy thing to understand, that when the scholar throws his arm over the neck of the horse to grab the bridle, the player immediately throws the arm to the scholar's neck, and with force makes him let go. You must do it as you see pictured here.

Questo sie un zogo di tore la brena d'lo cavallo de mane del compagno per modo che vedeti qui depento. Lo scolaro quando ello se scontra cum uno altro da cavallo, ello gli cavalca dela parte dritta, e butta gli lo suo brazo dritto per sopra lo collo dello cavalo, e pigla la sua brena apresso la sua man sinestra, cum la sua mane riversa. E tra la brena de la testa del cavallo. E questo zogo e piu siguro armado che disarmado.

This is a play of taking the bride of the horse from the companion's hand, in the way that you see drawn here. The scholar when he encounters with another on horseback, he rides to the right hand side, and throws his right arm over the horse's neck, and grabs the rein close to his [the opponent's] left hand, with his hand reversed [this probably means with the palm out, making the next action much easier]. And takes the reins off the horse's head. And this play is safer in armour than unarmoured.

WHAT'S NEXT?

You will have noticed that this book is not at all about *training*. Instead, I have tried to show you how I interpret Fiore's art, and why I do it the way I do it. For training purposes, I must direct you to my online course, hosted by me and Jessica Finley, at guywindsor.net/abrazarecourse

I am hard at work on similar volumes on Fiore's dagger section, and his armoured combat on foot. I hope to get at least one of those into your hands by 2025. I also teach in person at schools and seminars all over the world. To be kept informed of my seminar schedule and publishing efforts, you should join my mailing list. It's free, and there's never any spam. You can find it on my blog, at guywindsor.com.

If you have any questions or suggestions, feel free to email me at guy@guywindsor.com. It's always a pleasure hearing from readers – even when they have criticisms to offer!

GLOSSARY OF
ITALIAN TERMS

The list below includes words that are either unique to fencing manuscripts (Fiore's or Vadi's), or have a specific technical meaning in a fencing context. There are still some areas of debate among scholars of these arts; where I am aware of such, I have mentioned so in the comments. The translations are not necessarily applicable to modern Italian or other historical sources. Students should also note that the terms are often spelled several different ways in the original sources. Note that I have taken this from my book *The Art of Sword Fighting in Earnest*, and therefore several entries are specific to Vadi. I've noted them where they occur.

Italian grammar is quite simple, but has some aspects that English speakers may find odd – not least that a single word may have different forms, and to make a word plural, we can't just throw an 's' on the end. In general, nouns are either masculine or feminine, and adjectives will have both masculine and feminine forms that agree with the noun they describe. For example: *punta falsa*, false thrust; *filo falso*, false edge.

In general:

- Nouns ending in -e when singular will end in -i when plural: *fendente, fendenti.*
- Nouns ending in -o when singular will end in -i when plural: *colpo, colpi.*
- Nouns ending in -a when singular will end in -e when plural: *ligadura, ligadure.*

While it is standard practice to place all adjectives in their masculine form first, in the list below I have placed each word in the form that is most commonly used in Fiore (e.g. *longa*), and I have used the spellings that you will find in Fiore and/or Vadi's manuscripts, such as *zogho*, which would be *gioco* in modern Italian.

These terms are frequently combined: for example, *mandritto fendente* is a forehand descending blow.

Abrazare: To wrestle.

Accrescere: To step forwards without passing.

Audatia: Boldness. One of Fiore's four virtues. *Ardimento* in the Getty.

Avvisamento: Foresight. One of Fiore's four virtues. *Prudentia* in the Pisani-Dossi.

Bicorno: Two-horned. A guard.

Breve, posta breve: Short; short guard.

Celeritas: Speed. One of Fiore's four virtues. *Presteza* in the Getty.

Cinghiare / cinghiaro: Wild boar. The name of a specific guard position.

Colpo/i: blow(s) or strike(s).

Corona: Crown. The name of a specific guard position.

Coverta: Cover, parry.

Destro/a: On the right.

Discrescere: To step back without passing.

Donna: Woman or lady. The name of a specific guard position.

Dritto, diritto, derito: Right, forehand or true. *Filo* or *taglio dritto* is the true edge.

Elzo: Hilt; crossguard.

Falcon: Falcon. The name of a specific guard position (in Vadi).

Falso: False edge, back edge.

Fendente: Descending blow. Often qualified by *mandritto / dritto* (forehand) or *roverso* (backhand).

Finestra: Window. The name of a specific guard position.

Fora / for di strada: Out of the way. Often used in connection with a footwork action: thus *passo fora di strada*, 'pass out of the way'.

Fortitudo: Strength. One of Fiore's four virtues. *Forteza* in the Getty.

Frontale: Frontal, a guard.

Giocco / giocho / zogho: play. This is used to describe a single sequence (such as the first play of the sword) and, when qualified as *largo* or *stretto*, the tactical situation.

Giocco / giocho / zogho stretto: Close, narrow or constrained play. For a complete discussion, see pp196-208 of *The Longsword Plays of Fiore dei Liberi*.

Giocco / giocho / zogho largo: Wide play.

Incrosare / incroce: Crossing. Also parry.

Largo: Wide. Used in contrast to *stretto*. A state of play, or tactical situation, in which you are free to strike.

Ligadura: bind, usually an armlock. Can be upper, middle, or lower (*soprana, mezana, sottana*).

Lunga/Longa: Long.

Mandritto: Forehand. See *dritto / diritto*.

Mantener: Handle of the sword.

Meza spada / mezza spada: Half sword. A crossing made near the middle of both blades, and a grip of the sword, by handle and blade.

Mezana porta di ferro: Middle iron door. A guard position.

Mezano/i: Middle blows, horizontal blows.

Passare: To pass, as in stepping.

Passo: A pass, also the length of a passing step, also the space between your feet when standing.

Porta di ferro: Iron door. Can also be 'middle' (*mezana*) or 'whole' (*tutta*).

Posta / poste: Position or guard. Used more commonly than *guardia*.

Quatro dita: 'Four fingers.' A unit of measurement, the width of four fingers.

Rebattere: To beat aside – to parry.

Remedio: Remedy; the defence against an attack.

Rendopiare / reddopiare: Redouble. To strike again. Note: in 16th century Bolognese sources, *ridoppio* is a rising blow with the true edge, from the left. This is not the case here.

Riverso / roverso: Backhand.

Rompere: To break, as in the breaking of the thrust.

Rota: 'Turn', from *rotare*. A rising blow. Used by Vadi only.

Sagitaria: Archer; refers to specific guard positions, used differently by Fiore and Vadi.

Scambiare: To exchange, as in to exchange the thrust.

Sinestro: On the left.

Somesso: The width of a fist. A unit of measurement.

Sottano: A rising blow.

Stancho: Left (side or foot, usually). In modern Italian, 'tired'.

Strada: Way. This is used in the sense of the direct line between the two combatants. Hence to step *fora di strada*, 'out of the way', is to step off the line.

Stramazone: A whirling blow from the wrist.

Stretto / stretta / strette: Close, constrained, narrow. Used alone in plural form, *strette* means 'the *zogho stretto* plays of the sword'.

Taglio/e: Cut, and also cutting edge.

Traverso; ala traversa: Across, or diagonal. Usually used in connection with a footwork action: *va for de strada per traverso passo*, 'go out of the way with a pass across'.

Tondo: 'Round': a horizontal blow.

Tornare: 'To return'; to pass back.

Vera croce: True cross. A guard position (sword in armour).

Volta: Turn. Specifically *volta stabile* (stable turn: when with both feet fixed you can play on the same side in front and behind); *meza volta* (half turn: when with a pass forwards or backwards you can play on the other side); *tutta volta* (whole turn: when one foot remains fixed and the other turns around it).

Vista, visteggiare: Feint, to feint. (Fiore doesn't use it.)

Volante / volanti: 'Flying', a horizontal blow. This term is unique to Vadi.

Zenghiaro: Wild boar. A guard.

Zogho largo: Wide play. See *giocco largo*.

Zogho stretto: Close play. See *giocco stretto*.

BIBLIOGRAPHY

This is a short list of essential reading for any Fiore scholar, with a few interesting asides and extras.

Manuscript sources:

Fiore dei Liberi. *Il Fior di Battaglia*. MS Ludwig XV13. c.1400. J.P. Getty museum, Los Angeles. Available in facsimile from Spada Press, ISBN 978-9527157114.

Fiore dei Liberi. *Il Fior di Battaglia*. Morgan MS M 383. c.1400. New York: Pierpont Morgan Museum.

Fiore dei Liberi. *Florius de Arte Luctandi*. MS Latin 11269. c.1400. Paris: Bibliothèque Nationale de France.

Vadi, Philippo. *De Arte Gladiatoria Dimicandi*. MS Vitt. Em. 1324. 1482–1487. Rome: Biblioteca Nazionale. Available in facsimile from Spada Press, ISBN 978-9527157091, and in translation as Windsor, Guy. *The Art of Sword Fighting in Earnest*. Spada Press, 2018.

Modern editions of Fiore's work:

Chidester, Michael. *The Flower of Battle of Master Fiore Friulano de'i Liberi* (in two volumes). 2015. Retrieved 2 March 2017.

Novati, Francesco. *Flos Duellatorum in armis, sine armis, equester, pedester. Il Fior di Battaglia di Maestro Fiore dei Liberi da Premariacco*. Istituto Italiano d'Arte Grafiche, 1902.

Leoni, Tom, and Greg Mele. *Flowers of Battle Volume 1: historical overview and the Getty Manuscript*. Freelance Academy Press, 2017.

Fiore dei Liberi. *Il Fior di Battaglia: Ms Ludwig XV 13* (facsimile edition). Spada Press, 2017. ISBN: 978-9527157114

Hatcher, Colin, and Tracy Mellow. *The Flower of Battle: MS Ludwig XV13*. Tyrant Industries, 2017.

Leoni, Tom. *Fiore de' Liberi Fior di Battaglia Second English Edition*. Swordsman's Notebook, 2012.

Dictionaries:
Battaglia, Salvatore. *Grande Dizionario della lingua Italiana*. Turin: Unione tipografico-editrice torinese, 1961.

Cappelli, A. *Dizionario di Abbreviature Latine ed Italiane*. 1929. Retrieved 22 January 2024. https://archive.org/details/CappelliDizionarioDiAbbreviature.

Florio, John. *Queen Anna's New World of Words*. Edward Blount and William Barret, 1611.

Tommaseo, Nicolò. *Dizionario della Lingua Italiana*. Co-author Bernardo Bellini. 1861. Retrieved 13 April 2017. http://www.tommaseobellini.it.

Other cited works or reference resources:
Driscoll, M.J. *Electronic Textual Editing: Levels of transcription*. 2007. Retrieved 30 September 2015. http://www.tei-c.org/About/Archive_new/ETE/Preview/driscoll.xml

Fallows, Noel. *Jousting in Medieval and Renaissance Iberia*. Boydell Press, 2011.

Hagedorn, Dierk, and Bartłomiej Walczak. *Gladiatoria ~ New Haven – MS U860.F46 1450*. VS-Books, 2015.

Hagedorn, Dierk. *Jude Lew: Das Fechtbuch*. VS-Books, 2017.

Kaueper, Richard W., and Elspeth Kennedy. *The Book of Chivalry of Geoffroi de Charny: Text, Context, and Translation*. University of Pennsylvania Press, 1996.

Manciolino, Antonio. *Opera Nova*. Venice, 1531.

Mondschein, Ken. 'On the Art of Fighting: A Humanist Translation of Fiore dei Liberi's Flower of Battle Owned by Leonello D'Este', published in *Acta Periodica Duellatorum* volume 6 issue 1, 2018. https://ageaeditora.com/en/livros/apd006/.

Mondschein, Ken. *The Knightly Art of Battle*. Getty Publications, 2011.

Muhlberger, Steven. *Deeds of Arms*. Chivalry Bookshelf, 2005.

Muhlberger, Steven. *Royal Jousts at the End of the Fourteenth Century*. Freelance Academy Press, 2012.

Muhlberger, Steven. *Formal Combats in the Fourteenth Century*. Witan Press, 2013.

Oakeshott, Ewart. *Records of the Medieval Sword.* The Boydell Press, 1991.

Tobler, Christian. *Fighting with the German Longsword.* Freelance Academy Press, 2016.

Viggiani, Angelo. *Lo Schermo.* Venice, 1575. Published in translation as Swanger, W. Jherek. *The Fencing Method of Angelo Viggiani: Lo Schermo, Part III.* Lulu Press, 2018. For fencers, part III is the important bit; parts I and II can be skipped.

Windsor, Guy. 'Half Full? Translating Mezza and Tutta in Il Fior di Battaglia'. 2006. See https://guywindsor.net/free-resources

Windsor, Guy. 'Finding Bicorno'. 2008. See https://guywindsor.net/free-resources

Windsor, Guy. *The Armizare Vade Mecum.* Freelance Academy Press, 2011.

Windsor, Guy. *Mastering the Art of Arms, Book 1: The Medieval Dagger.* Freelance Academy Press, 2012.

Windsor, Guy. *Mastering the Art of Arms, Book 2: The Medieval Longsword.* The School of European Swordsmanship, 2014.

Windsor, Guy. *Mastering the Art of Arms, Book 3: Advanced Longsword, Form and Function.* The School of European Swordsmanship, 2016.

Windsor, Guy. *The Art of Sword Fighting in Earnest.* Spada Press, 2018.

Windsor, Guy. *Recreating Medieval and Renaissance European combat systems: A Critical Review of* The Art of Sword Fighting in Earnest, Mastering the Art of Arms volume 1: The Medieval Dagger, *and* The Duellist's Companion. The University of Edinburgh, 2018.

Windsor, Guy. *From Medieval Manuscript To Modern Practice: the Longsword Techniques of Fiore dei Liberi,* 2020

Zabinski, Grzegorz, and Bartłomiej Walczak. *Codex Wallerstein: A Medieval Fighting Book from the Fifteenth Century on the Longsword, Falchion, Dagger, and Wrestling.* Paladin Press, 2002.

Zanutto, Luigi. *Fiore dei Liberi da Premariacco e i ludi e le festi marziali in Friuli nel Medio-evo.* Del Bianco, 1907.

ABOUT THE AUTHOR

Dr Guy Windsor is a world-renowned instructor and a pioneering researcher of medieval and Renaissance martial arts. He has been teaching the art of arms full time since founding the School of European Swordsmanship in Helsinki, Finland, in 2001. His day job is finding and analysing historical swordsmanship treatises, figuring out the systems they represent, creating a syllabus from the treatises for his students to train with, and teaching the system to his students all over the world. Guy is the author of numerous classic books about the art of swordsmanship and has consulted on swordfighting game design and stage combat. He developed the card game Audatia, based on Fiore dei Liberi's art of arms, his primary field of study. In 2018 Edinburgh University awarded him a PhD by research publications for his work recreating historical combat systems. When not studying medieval and renaissance swordsmanship or writing books, Guy can be found in his shed woodworking or spending time with his family.

FROM THE SAME AUTHOR

If you've enjoyed this book you should definitely visit swordschool. com and sign up for my newsletter. There's never any spam, and you'll get the news first about new releases and giveaways.

You may also like the following:

On Fiore's Art of Arms:

The Armizare Workbook, part one: Beginners Course [https:// guywindsor.net/awb1] This workbook includes detailed instruction, videos, and (in the printed versions) space for notes. It also allows the student to choose their own path through the material, with options presented at every stage.

Mastering the Art of Arms, Book 1: The Medieval Dagger [https:// www.guywindsor.net/dagger] A training manual for Fiore's dagger techniques. This is a complete overview of the dagger material in Fiore's art of arms, and includes instruction on how to fall, how to develop real skills, as well as covering all of the fundamental attacks with and defences against the dagger. Hardback available from Spada Press, paperback and ebook from Freelance Academy Press.

Mastering the Art of Arms, Book 2: The Medieval Longsword. A training manual for Fiore's longsword plays. If you want to learn how to train and fight with a longsword in an authentic medieval style, this book is for you. This book features an introduction by the excellent historical novelist and medieval combatant, Christian Cameron.

Mastering the Art of Arms, Book 3: Advanced Longsword, Form and Function This covers using forms for skill development, and a lot of Fiore-specific training, building on the groundwork laid in *The Medieval Longsword.*

From Medieval Manuscript to Modern Practice: the Longsword Techniques of Fiore dei Liberi. This has my transcription, translation, commentary, and links to video clips of my interpretation of all of Fiore's longsword plays on foot out of armour, as well as a thorough introduction.

The Swordsman's Companion. A training manual for medieval longsword. This was my first book, and it has become something of a classic in this field. As a training manual, it is largely replaced by *The Medieval Longsword*, but as a book about how and why to train, it is still relevant.

The Armizare Vade Mecum. Mnemonic verses for remembering Fiore's art. This is a collection of verses, each one of which encapsulates one element of Fiore's art.

On Vadi's Art of Arms:

The Art of Sword Fighting in Earnest. An accurate translation of Filippo Vadi's *De Arte Gladiatoria Dimicandi,* with a detailed introduction, commentary from a practical swordsmanship perspective, and a full glossary. This book was examined as part of my PhD, so it's been academically vetted at the highest level.

If you prefer to learn from audio or video, check out my online courses at https://courses.swordschool.com

On Historical Martial Arts:

The Theory and Practice of Historical Martial Arts. [https://guywindsor. net/tandp] This book includes all seven instalments of *The Swordsman's Quick Guide,* as well as extensive instruction on recreating historical martial arts from historical sources, how to train, how to teach, even how to get better sleep.

Swordfighting, for Writers, Game Designers, and Martial Artists. [https://guywindsor.net/sgg] This book is made up of about 50% posts from my blog and 50% new material, and does exactly what it says in the title. It also features an introduction from the one and only Neal Stephenson, author of *Snow Crash, The Diamond Age,* and *The Baroque Cycle,* to name but a few.

On Training in General

The Principles and Practices of Solo Training: [https://guywindsor.net/book/windsormethod] the self-help book for people who want to add years to their life and life to their years. In this refreshingly straight-forward and gentle guide I lay out the fundamental principles behind personal development and excellence in any field. How? By establishing a solid foundation, and a step-by-step approach to mechanics and training. Use this book to guide your practice and elevate your skills.

On Capoferro's Rapier method:

The Rapier Workbooks:

These workbooks comprise a complete training method for becoming proficient at Capoferro's style of rapier fencing. Each workbook is designed to lie flat, with abundant space for note-taking, and with a linked video clip for every action. They are available laid out for right or left handers, to make note-taking easier.

The Rapier Workbook Part 1, Beginners (you can get the ebook version free at guywindsor.net/tdcextras)
The Rapier Workbook Part 2, Completing the Basics
The Rapier Workbook Part 3, Developing Your Skills
The Rapier Workbook Part 4, Sword and Dagger and Sword and Cape

I have also compiled the four workbooks into one volume, The Complete Rapier Workbook. [https://guywindsor.net/rw5]

ACKNOWLEDGMENTS

In the course of researching Fiore's wonderful art, I have had the support and assistance of hundreds of students, and many colleagues. Chief among the latter, in terms of researching Fiore, would be Greg Mele, Tom Leoni, and Sean Hayes, with whom I have had many stimulating discussions, and who never just take my word for anything academic. A special nod to Sean Manning who wrote critical reviews of a couple of my previous works that helped inspire this series.

Most of the videos have been extracted from my Abrazare Course material, so special thanks to Jessica Finley, who assisted me on the course and added her depth of knowledge and experience to the work. I must also thank her for her direct contribution to this book, the All Work and No Play chapter.

I would also like to thank my indefatigable assistant, Katie Mackenzie for handling much of the pernicketyness that comes with being a writer, and my editors: Andrew Chapman, who streamlined the work greatly, and my mother Maxine Windsor for a final proof-reading polish. Any errors are my own, of course!

Thank you all!

Guy

Made in the USA
Las Vegas, NV
03 October 2024

96137458R10105